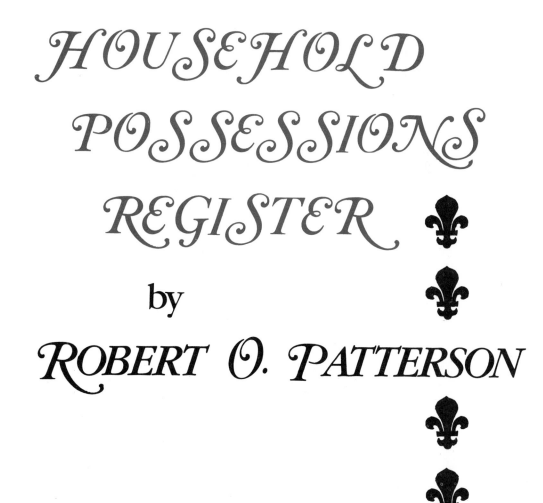

HOUSEHOLD POSSESSIONS REGISTER

by

ROBERT O. PATTERSON

POPLAR BOOKS

Manufactured in the United States of
America

Designed by
BARBARA LEVINE

ISBN No: 0-89009-355-5

TABLE OF CONTENTS

THE REGISTER

How To Use This Register Of Personal Possessions

You have in your hands one of the best security records available. If you use it properly and keep it up to date, it will eliminate much trouble and anguish in case of disaster.

RECORDING POSSESSIONS • If you are typical, you have no accurate inventory of your personal possessions. That's what this Register is for. By listing your personal possessions in appropriate categories, you will have a permanent record which can be used in case of loss or damage by fire, flood, windstorm, burglary, vandalism, etc.

These events may not occur, but your Register will be an ideal record for warranty purposes; for example, if you require repairs or servicing for electronic or mechanical items, having the model and serial numbers recorded will facilitate service.

LOSS AND DAMAGE • In addition to providing you with an up-to-date inventory of your major possessions, this Register has introductory sections on insuring your possessions, protecting your possessions, improving home security, and what to do if you suffer loss from natural perils or burglary. There is also a section on personal liability coverage and the tax advantages to be gained.

The information in this Register is to be considered for use as guidelines only. Provisions of insurance coverage, security requirements, and legal liability vary from state to state and are constantly changing. The material on insurance should be checked with your local insurance agent; home security methods should be verified with local law enforcement agencies. This register is not a substitute for carefully reading one's policies.

KEEPING YOUR RECORDS SAFE • The ideal place to safeguard this inventory of your possessions is in a bank safe-deposit box.

Special fire retardant record boxes or files may also be purchased from office equipment and supply dealers. These are heavy steel boxes or file cabinets which have a thick layer of asbestos or other fire retardant material between inner and outer walls of steel. Less desirable are "safes" which have a water jacket between the outer and inner walls. In fire tests a number of these "safes" have leaked the fluid and the interior contents have been incinerated.

Of course, none of the above offers the protection of the safe-deposit box.

*I*mproving Your ⚜ Home's Security

Whether you live in a house, a town house or an apartment, security is an increasingly important consideration. A good security system not only contributes to peace of mind, it may prevent expensive loss of property and even threat against life, as well.

TYPES OF SECURITY • There are two main types of security: perimeter and area. "Perimeter security" means preventing, discouraging or detecting intrusion from outside the dwelling. "Area security" means detecting and discouraging intruders who have gained entry to the dwelling.

The most common devices for perimeter security are the door lock and the window catch. Most houses and many apartments are surprisingly easy to break into. The average burglar is not a professional. He is more likely to be a youth with minimal experience, looking for something expensive and portable to be turned into cash quickly. Such things as stereos, television sets (particularly portables), jewelry and cameras are particularly sought.

As a result, the amateur or casual burglar generally thinks of entering through a door, even though windows may be much easier to open. If door locks are secure and resistant to opening by the methods usually employed, the inexperienced burglar may be deterred and discouraged.

There are four commonly used methods of entry by most unsophisticated burglars. These are: prying, hammering, cutting, and kicking. The prybar, often called a "jimmy," is the most common prying tool. Large screwdrivers are also used. Prying has the advantage — to the burglar — of being a quick, relatively quiet method, and the tool can be easily concealed in clothing.

Hammering is also effective, but it's noisy, and most burglars will only do it to break glass to reach a lock or catch, or, in frustration, when other methods don't work. Cutting is generally used only when a door has a hasp type of lock and the hacksaw can be easily employed.

Kicking, surprisingly, is the most widely used and most effective method of gaining entry, particularly when the door and the jambs are wood. The human kick has great force, and is relatively quiet. From the burglar's standpoint, it is preferred because it does not require incriminating tools.

BETTER DOOR LOCKS • The two most common types of door locks for outside entry are the mortise lock and the key-in-knob. Neither of these is good protection and should probably be backed up with an auxiliary lock of the deadbolt type. Both the mortise lock, which is a cylinder fitted into a hole bored into the outside surface of the door, and the key-in-knob lock can be easily pulled out of the door with modest tools and the door mechanism turned with a screwdriver. In addition, both of these locks usually have unreinforced strike plates (into which the latch or bolt fits) which may be pulled out of a wooden door jamb with a simple kick against the door.

The simplest type of auxiliary lock to install is a vertical deadbolt lock. This lock fits on the inside of the door with a cylinder reaching through a hole to the outside surface. The only weakness of this type of lock is the strike, which must be installed on the inside surface of the jamb. For maximum security, the strike must have screws of at least three inches long, which reach into the stud under the jamb.

EFFECTIVE WINDOW CATCHES • Most types of window catches and locks are bolted onto the surface of the sash of the double-hung window. With the aid of a jimmy or a large screwdriver, the average window can be opened in a matter of seconds by prying up the bottom sash, ripping the latch or lock from the wood. Even the wedge type "ventilating" lock is "wiped" off the edge of the sash by a strong pry. The best way to secure windows is to drill a hole through the bottom sash into the top sash where they overlap and insert a 1/4" cap screw or eyebolt on each side of the window.

However, the problem with windows is that they may be easily broken and larger sizes permit direct entry.

BURGLAR ALARMS •

The best method of discouraging burglars is to make it too noisy for them to hang around to finish their burglary. That's the way most burglar alarms work. They set up an unholy clamor when the burglar trips them. This applies to both perimeter and area types. Another type makes no sound in the dwelling, but transmits an alert to a police station or private security office.

Burglar alarms may be extremely elaborate systems which require experts to install and which cost a great deal, or they may be relatively simple devices which you may install yourself.

PERIMETER ALARMS •

The most common burglar alarm is some kind of perimeter warning. When a window is opened or a door forced, the alarm goes off. The system includes switches on each door and window to be protected, wire to connect them to a central box, and an alarm bell or siren. Most systems work on either house current or battery power. Some have an anti-tamper circuit to sound an alarm when an intruder tries to cut the house power.

There are also more complex and expensive systems of perimeter security which require no wires between the opening to be protected and the central box. Instead, a transmitter at each opening sends a message to the central box if the door or window is opened. And there are less expensive systems which involve only a small unit being hung on a door knob or attached to the bottom of a door. These battery-powered devices sound off if anyone opens the door.

Both home-installed and specialist-installed systems are available with automatic dialing devices which notify police or a private security office that someone is breaking into the dwelling. Because of the number of false alarms — particularly in households with children — some areas prohibit the use of these devices to warn police. Most systems of this type do not use an audible alarm to warn away intruders, but depend upon the quick reaction of police or security guards to apprehend them.

AREA ALARMS •

There are different types of area alarms. Some detect intruders who have already entered the dwelling. One of the simplest and most effective for an apartment which has a long entry hall is a runner which sounds an alarm when trod upon. Photoelectric cells may also be used, with some of the more basic of these devices simple small boxes which plug into an ordinary electrical outlet, with the reflecting mirror (which has an adhesive back) fastened to an opposite wall.

The more common of the area alarms, however, is either ultrasonic or microwave actuated. These devices put out a beam across a room or other area. When anything moves into the beam, it sets off the alarm. Most of these devices operate off house current, with some models also utilizing battery power.

When installing an alarm system, be sure to check if your community has a law regulating the amount of time a burglar alarm may sound. All systems are available with alarms which sound for a given period, usually five minutes, and then reset themselves again.

DON'T INVITE BURGLARS •

If your house is to be vacant for some time — for example, when you are on vacation — be sure that the mail is stopped, deliveries of newspapers are cut off, and someone drops by periodically to pick up flyers and other throwaways which indicate that the resident is absent.

You may also wish to give the appearance of someone living in the house. This can be accomplished by installing several small, inexpensive electric timers attached to lamps. By phasing the on and off times, it can appear as if the family starts off in the kitchen, moves to the family room and finally to bed.

To confuse possible burglars who might be casing the house, "variable" timers are available, which vary the on and off times slightly from one time to the next.

If you are going to be away, some police departments, upon notification, will patrol in your area to look over the place carefully on each swing. Ask neighbors to note any suspicious activity, such as cars in the driveway or in front, or lights (other than yours) in the house at night. In fact, if you are using timers, the absence of lighting in the evening may be a tipoff that something is wrong.

One of the best methods to protect your house when you are away is to have a neighbor make a circuit around the house each day to see if the windows and doors are securely closed. And be sure to instruct them to call the police if they find signs of entry. The earlier the police find out about a burglary, the better chance of recovery of the stolen items.

ELIMINATE HIDING PLACES • If you live in a well-lighted city area or in a suburb with houses in close proximity to the street, be sure you are not providing havens for burglars. Such hiding places as large shrubs which screen windows or doors on the ground floor are a natural place to make a break-in. Large trees which have branches brushing against the house near windows are an easy ladder to an upper-story by an agile burglar. Fancy trellises fastened to the side of the house can often be used as a route to a second story where entry is generally easier than on the ground floor.

Precautions Against Perils

While no one can accurately forecast when a peril will strike, there are some things you can do to reduce the loss which would be caused by flood, fire, burglary, etc. These precautions should be considered a type of insurance against possible damage.

FLOODED BASEMENTS • One of the biggest causes of loss for most homeowners with basements is water from the surrounding soil rising in the winter or spring when rains are heavy and the ground water table rises. A suitable precaution would be to install a sump pump in a shallow well at the lowest part of the basement. Today's automatic sump pumps activate when four inches of water collect in the sump.

Also, it is a sensible precaution to store boxes and other containers at least 12 inches above the floor. Simple, inexpensive wood racks can be built to hold stored objects off the floor. These will also make it easier to clean the basement. Make sure your furnace and appliances are at least 6 inches above the basement floor.

ATTIC LEAKS • Another favorite place for storage in a home is the attic. If the roof leaks, this is the first place to be soaked. Therefore, it makes sense to keep objects stored in the attic covered with plastic sheets, weighted down around the edges. These will also keep dust from settling on the stored items.

SMOKE AND FLAME ALARMS • Within the past few years, the price of smoke and flame alarms has dropped to the point where these devices have become one of the least expensive security systems available. Install one of each on the main floor of the house, a flame (heat) alarm near the kitchen, and a smoke alarm in the hallway outside the bedrooms. Install a smoke alarm in the basement in the stairwell leading to the main floor if you have a gas, oil, or coal furnace in the basement. Install smoke alarms on upper floors at the top of stairwells.

Most alarms operate on self-contained batteries, with indicators telling when batteries have become exhausted. Ones which operate on house current have the disadvantage that an electrical fire might destroy house current before the alarm senses the smoke or heat.

ELIMINATE LITTER • "Spontaneous" combustion may seem unlikely, but many household fires are caused by just such a condition. The worst offenders are oil or grease-soaked rags wadded up and placed in a closet or cabinet. Another dangerous condition are collections of old newspapers or magazines. Also, woodchips and shavings, or heaps of sawdust left over from construction might not start a fire in themselves, but will speed the spread of flames in a fire.

Put out traps for mice if there are any signs of infestation. When mice − and squirrels − gnaw on electric wire insulation to get material for nests, fire often occurs.

Don't store paint thinners, flammable cleaning fluids, gasoline, etc., in the house, or in the garage. The place for these potentially dangerous fluids is in a separate structure, detached and apart from either house or garage. A small tool shed or a doghouse would be best. It's also a good idea to place oil-based paints in the same separate storage. Sealed, these are not fire hazards, but in a fire, they tend to explode and spread the flames.

POISONS • If you have children, or if children ever come to visit, insure that all poisons, including such things as bowl cleaners, drain cleaners, insecticides, chlorine, lye, etc., are placed not in the usual under-the-sink cabinets, but above a child's reach. And make sure that every one of these dangerous compounds has a child-proof closure.

These precautions will prevent anguish and possible lawsuits.

ANTICIPATING THEFT • The type of item which the average burglar seeks is the portable television set, the stereo set or components, cameras, portable radios, jewelry, etc. These are items which can be carried off fairly easily and which are converted quickly to cash through a fence or by selling on the street.

One way to make such fencing or sale more risky for the burglar is to mark each such item indelibly. If your community has a program of registering and marking equipment of this sort, get a number from the local police. If there is not such a program use your social security number and inscribe it on a metal or plastic surface of the device − preferably metal − with an "electric pencil," an inexpensive device which engraves the number on almost any type of surface.

While this marking will not prevent theft, it makes the likelihood of recovery much better than if there is no identification.

FIREARMS AND AMMUNITION • If you have firearms in your home, they are not only a favorite target of burglars, but they could possibly cause major liability exposure. Be sure to safeguard firearms.

EXPERTS RECOMMEND THREE SECURITY STEPS:

1. Insure that all firearms are unloaded. (If you own a decorator muzzle loader heirloom, it would be wise to take it to a gunsmith to check for old charges loaded and forgotten.)

2. Secure each firearm with a trigger lock. These inexpensive devices fit through the trigger guard of all except lever-action rifles and lock securely with a key to prevent trigger movement.

3. Lock all firearms in a closet or cabinet where children cannot get at them.

Ammunition must also be safeguarded. Experts recommend that ammunition *not* be stored with the firearms. They recommend storing it in a locked cabinet or closet away from heat or possible sources of fire.

Do not buy excessive ammunition. With age, the explosive may change characteristics. Older ammunition may misfire, explode with greater force than when fresh, or even become sensitive to shock.

PHOTOGRAPHING YOUR POSSESSIONS • One of the best supporting evidences of your possessions is a set of detailed color photographs. You can take these yourself without expensive cameras or equipment.

Here's how: Indoors use a flash. Stand at one side of a larger room and photograph the opposite wall. Then move around the room, photographing each wall in order. For a smaller room, stand in the corner and be sure only one wall appears in your viewfinder. Repeat in each corner.

Outdoors, stand back and photograph each wall, making sure to include the complete roof if it shows from the ground. Then photograph the yard, standing well back from trees to include as much foliage as possible.

This set of photographs should be updated (new ones taken) at least every other year. In addition to verifying the existence and condition of your house (or apartment) and furnishings, the photos will provide an excellent record of additions, alterations, and refurbishings of your dwelling for insurance and tax purposes.

OVERLOADING CIRCUITS • One cause of home fires is overloaded circuits. If lights dim or cords get hot, you have overloaded the circuit, and a fire could start. Be sure that you have adequate electrical service into your home. Some older homes have inadequate power supplied from the utility lines. *Never* replace a burned-out fuse by placing a metal coin or slug under it. Don't run wires under rugs where insulation will wear. Make sure large appliances, particularly air conditioners, use heavy duty extension cords no longer than required.

FIREPLACES AND WOOD STOVES • Whenever burning a fire in a fireplace, use a fire screen to prevent flying sparks. A glass fire screen will prevent sparks and conserve energy by preventing room air from being drawn out through the chimney. Make sure fireplace and furnace chimneys are cleaned regularly. A partially blocked chimney can catch fire. A fully blocked one can cause toxic fumes to back up into the house. Be aware that many fireplaces built since 1900 are constructed primarily for decorative purposes and are not designed to be burned continuously over long periods of time. Doing so can cause a fire. Today, with the dramatic increase in home heating costs, many people are using their fireplaces much more than they were designed to be used. Ask your local fire department to check your fireplace if you have any doubts as to its safety or construction. Never leave a fire burning in the fireplace or old-fashioned wood stove when you go to bed or leave the house.

If you have installed one of the popular wood burning stoves, have it inspected by the local fire department to be sure it meets the fire code for safety. Wood stoves and kerosene heaters use up oxygen. Never use a wood stove or kerosene heater in a room with the door shut. You will go out long before the flames will.

Store matches out of reach of children!

TOT SAVERS • Some local fire departments supply free stickers to be placed in windows of children's rooms so firemen can identify those rooms and check children's safety first.

SMOKING HAZARDS • Don't smoke in bed. Don't place ashtrays on upholstered furniture. Don't empty ashtrays into waste baskets or trash bags.

CHRISTMAS • Don't leave lights burning on the tree overnight or when you leave the house. Paper and gift wrappings should be taken outside to the trash immediately after presents are opened.

Watch out for papers and children around the fireplace.

Be sure toys and other plastic objects are not placed on radiators or in front of hot air registers.

Insuring Your Personal Possessions

(The following information on homeowners insurance policies is general and for use as guidelines only. Each insurance company has variations from the standard form and coverage varies from state to state and area to area. Ask your insurance agent about the coverage, exclusions, and limitations to your policy — and read the policy carefully!)

If you are typical, you have your household possessions insured against fire and theft under a "homeowners policy," whether you own a home or not. If you don't have insurance, now is the time to get it, for inflation is pushing up the replacement cost of everything you own — and your potential loss is getting bigger every month.

Getting insurance is not difficult in most parts of the country, but the cost varies considerably. If you live in a suburban area with a history of little crime and a good fire department nearby, your insurance costs (per $1,000) will probably be low. If you live in a central city with a high crime rate, and you are on the upper floors of a tall apartment house, your rates will probably be high. In some such areas, you may not be able to get regular homeowners insurance at all, but will have to turn to the government for Federal Crime Insurance. In some areas, where fire is a major risk, you may have to turn to FAIR (Fair Access to Insurance Requirements), which is Federal government backed.

A typical situation where FAIR would be required is a house on a brush-covered hillside, or one in a forest area subject to forest fires. Like all other types of insurance, homeowners policy rates are based upon the companies' experience. Where their experience shows that risk is high, they charge higher premiums. Where their experience shows that risk is so high that adequate premiums cannot be charged, they generally refuse to issue policies. That's when the government has stepped in and provided either insurance or financial backing to the insurance companies. Federal Crime Insurance is directly provided by the government. FAIR is provided by insurance companies with the costs underwritten by Federal backing.

Homeowners policies are an excellent way to cover everything you own (except for automobiles, other vehicles, aircraft, and boats). However, they are not the ideal insurance for your big investments in jewelry, furs, coins, stamps, antiques, etc. If you have such valuable possessions — even several good cameras and lenses, plus electronic flash and filters, homeowners insurance is inadequate.

HOMEOWNERS PROTECTION ● First, let's look at what homeowners insurance does protect you against.

— It will protect you if you are a homeowner, a renter (of either a house or an apartment) or an owner of a condominium.

— It will protect you against fire, theft, lightning, windstorm, and a number of other perils listed in the table.

— It will protect your house, outbuildings, and shrubbery if you are a homeowner or condominium owner.

— It will protect you against damage or theft losses for personal property in your home and to some extent for property away from your home.

In addition, homeowners policies cover your living expenses away from home when you have to move out because of damage to your residence and its contents. It will also protect you against:

— Personal liability claims against you, your family, and persons under the age of 21 living with you. Claims might occur when a passerby trips on your uneven sidewalk or falls down a flight of stairs in your home; if your dog bites someone passing you on the street, or if you inadvertently hurt someone at golf, tennis, archery, etc.

— It provides medical expenses for persons you injure.

— It provides protection against damage you cause to the property of others, such as a tree falling on a neighbor's house, or water from your overflowing bathtub ruining your downstairs neighbor's rugs.

But homeowners policy coverage is hedged by various exceptions, restrictions, and limits. You must know exactly what you are covered for. And you may have to back up your homeowners policy with other insurance coverage, such as "floaters," on certain valuable possessions which are not covered fully in your homeowners policy. These exclusions, conditions, and limits are listed in the table.

TYPES OF HOMEOWNERS INSURANCE • There are six basic types of homeowners insurance, plus two special types which have been recently introduced by a number of companies, but which are not available in all states as yet.

HO-1 is the least expensive of the homeowners policies. It is less expensive because it does not provide as much coverage as other policies. (See table) It is not issued by all companies.

HO-2 has better coverage, but it also lacks some of the protection of the "standard" type of homeowners insurance written by most companies.

HO-3 is the so-called "standard" policy, issued by most companies. It protects against a broad range of perils. (See table)

HO-4 is a policy for renters, either of houses or apartments. It has basically the same protection level as HO-3, except that it does not protect the house or apartment, merely personal and household possessions.

HO-5 is the broadest coverage policy for homeowners. It is known as an all-risk policy, and has fewer exclusions and limitations than the HO-3. It is also the most expensive.

HO-6 is the policy for condominium owners. Limits include $1,000 on owner's additions and alterations to the condo unit.

Two new forms have been recently introduced by some companies in some states. These have not yet been given HO code numbers. Both are intended for homeowners of properties which are old and sound, but which could not sell for the cost of replacing them. Basically, each policy reduces the coverage. One version was developed by the National Association of Independent Insurers. It calls for replacement with commonly used construction materials instead of duplicating the original construction. This might mean repair with drywall instead of three-coat plaster and wooden lath.

The second version was introduced by the Insurance Services Office, which represents another group of insurance companies. It calls for all losses to be paid at actual cash value, but not to exceed in total the cost of repair or replacement. A warning with this policy is that it limits reimbursement for any one theft to $1,000 — hardly enough considering the cost of today's televisions, stereos, etc.

Nevertheless, for homeowners with old houses and a problem in getting insurance, these new policies may be the only solution.

REIMBURSEMENT • How do the insurance companies figure reimbursement? Two ways, one on the structure(s) and one on the personal property (household possessions) contained on the premises.

For reimbursement for a house itself, it depends upon whether the damage is partial or total. For complete reimbursement of a partial loss — such as a kitchen fire — you must have at least 80%

coverage of the full replacement cost of the house. That means that the face value of your policy must be at least 80% of what it would cost to rebuild the complete building from the foundation up.

If you have the 80% coverage, you will get complete reimbursement of your costs for repair or replacement of the partial damage. If you have less than 80%, you will get a pro rata reimbursement. For example, if your home would cost $80,000 to replace and you had it insured for $60,000, you would be insured for only 75% of the value. If your kitchen burned and repairs (to the structure, not the appliances, dishes, etc.) cost $3,000, the insurance company would pay you only $2,250, 75% of the cost of replacement. On the other hand, if you had insurance of $64,000 or more (80% of the cost of replacement) they would pay the full amount of the partial repairs or replacement — $3,000.

If your house is completely destroyed, however, you will find the insurance company will pay no more than the face value of the policy. In the same case, if the house cost $80,000 to replace, and you had it insured for 80% ($64,000), you would receive only $64,000 against the cost.

Personal possessions are another story. They are reimbursed on the "actual cash value" of the possession. In our case above, the kitchen sustained $3,000 damage to the structure — that is, walls, ceilings, floors, built in cabinets, electrical wiring, and plumbing. In addition, the stove (original cost $300, four years old, with replacement cost $450) and the refrigerator next to it (original cost $415, one year old, replacement cost $475) were damaged and required replacement.

Most insurance companies would figure your reimbursement on this basis: both stove and refrigerator would be considered to have a useful life of 10 years. The replacement cost of the stove is $450 for a similar model by the same manufacturer, or a similar one with the same features. The reimbursement would be figured at 6/10ths of the $450, or a reimbursement of $270. In the case of the refrigerator, the replacement cost is $475, and you would receive 9/10ths of the cost: $427.50.

COVERAGE UNDER HOMEOWNERS POLICIES • The perils covered under a
homeowners policy may vary slightly from state to state and from company to company, but basically they are the same, depending upon the HO contract used.

HO-1 covers a limited number of perils. (See table) It requires a minimum $8,000 coverage on the house. Detached structures (garage, tool shed, cabanas) are covered up to 10% of the amount of insurance on the house. Trees and shrubs are covered up to 5% of the amount on the house, with a maximum of $250 for any one tree, plant, shrub, etc. Personal property (see table) is covered up to 50% of the amount of insurance on the house. Additional living expenses are limited to 10% of the amount of insurance on the house.

HO-2 covers a more extensive list of perils. (See table) All other limits of coverage are the same as HO-1 except for additional living expense, which is up to 20% of the amount of insurance on the house.

HO-3 covers all perils (see table) on personal property except glass breakage. It covers all risk, except those specifically excluded, for the house and other structures. Coverage limits are the same as for HO-2.

HO-4 has coverage similar to HO-3, except there is no coverage of the building or detached structures. There is, however, insurance on renter-performed additions and alterations to the unit or house, up to 10% of the value of personal property insurance. Trees, plants, and shrubs are covered up to 10% of the value of the personal property insurance with a maximum of $250 per tree or shrub. Personal property coverage must be a minimum of $4,000. Personal property away from the premises is covered to the extent of 10% of the value of the personal property insurance, but there is a $1,000 minimum coverage required. Additional living expense is 20% of the personal property insurance.

HO-5, the so-called "all risk" policy, covers all risk, except those specifically excluded. The minimum amount of insurance offered is $15,000. All other coverage is similar to HO-3, except that coverage of personal property away from the premises is 50% of the value of the house insurance.

HO-6, like HO-4, does not provide insurance on structure or detached buildings (which are generally carried as part of the condominium's management services) but it provides coverage up to $1,000 on owner's additions and alterations to the unit. All other coverage is similar to HO-4, except that additional living expenses are covered up to 40% of the value of the personal property insurance.

All standard forms, HO-1 through HO-6, provide the same special limits of liability (see table), $25,000 coverage of personal liability, $250 property damage coverage for possessions of others, and medical payments of $500 per person, up to $25,000 for all injured in the same accident.

DEDUCTIBLES •
Deductibles are one area of homeowners insurance where the buyer must beware. Some policies have deductibles built in. Others make them available if the insured wants them. Why deductibles?

Deductibles are a form of minor "self insurance." In the policy, where the deductible is at the discretion of the insured, by insuring yourself for the first $100 or $250 of each loss, you are able to get lower premium rates than if you can collect every dollar. This is limited self insurance. You are, in effect, saying, "I'm going to assume the risk myself for small losses, and use the insurance for major losses."

In those policies, however, which have the deductible built in, there is often no apparent reduction in premium. The company has decided to pass the risk on to the insured, and you are not even aware of it, in most cases, since many agents don't stress such deductibles. They are usually buried in the small print. Insurance companies explain away built in deductibles as "nuisance prevention." They explain that the costs of servicing small claims would raise the rate on homeowners insurance higher than most people would tolerate.

A typical built in deductible phrasing is, "With respect to loss covered under this policy, this company shall be liable only when such loss in each occurrence exceeds $50. When loss is between $50 and $500 this company shall be liable for 111% of loss in excess of $50 and when loss is $500 or more, this loss deductible clause shall not apply. This loss deductible clause shall not apply to…additional living expense or fire department service charge."

Such a deductible is generally removable from the coverage by the payment of an additional premium, which leads some to believe that such limitations are another method of increasing the income from policies without raising rates.

On the other hand, many wish to self insure for small losses. That is, if it results in lowering the cost of the policy. Deductibles often are reduced on the basis of good experience, although the rates do not go up. One such policy says, "In addition, this amount shall be reduced ten dollars ($10) for each successive continuous twelve-month period the insured has not sustained a loss under this policy subject to the deductible. The maximum reduction under this clause shall be fifty dollars ($50)."

Deductibles are not applied to additional living expense, fire department service charge, or to certain supplementary coverage, such as credit card loss or depositors forgery coverage where they are offered.

CALCULATING COVERAGE •
How do you go about figuring out how much the insurance policy should be? What is the full replacement value of your home? Or, if you are an apartment or condominium dweller, how much would total replacement of your personal possessions cost?

For a house, there is less of a problem. The insurance agent has a table of construction costs in your area. By measuring the square footage of the house (outside measurements), he can quickly convert the size of the house to the proper chart for the type of construction (frame, brick, stucco, etc.). However, this cost rapidly changes. Not only do ordinary inflation factors become involved, but labor costs may change drastically from year to year.

Some insurance experts say that the replacement value of a house should be recalculated every other year. Some say every year. And insurance companies have a special provision to keep up with inflation (or at least not to fall too far behind) called an "inflation guard." This is an automatic raising of the value of coverage every year on policies HO-1, HO-2, HO-3, and HO-5. It calls for the raising of the limits of liability by 1% at the end of each 3-month period. This, of course, is not free. There is an increased premium involved with the increase. But it does help to keep from falling too far behind inflation.

If you are a renter or a condominium owner, or a homeowner who wishes to be sure your personal possessions do not total more than 50% of the value of the house, calculating your replacement value of personal possessions can be difficult. The first step, of course, is to make a complete listing of all items. This Register is an ideal method of keeping that record of item, date acquired, cost, and any model or serial number. Ideally, after getting a complete inventory of each item, calculate how much it would cost to replace it with an identical or similar item, then reduce that figure by the depreciation and add all of the amounts together to get the "actual cash value" of all of your possessions.

Lifetimes for various possessions may be found in Publication 534, "Tax Information on Depreciation," published by the Internal Revenue Service, and free from the IRS Forms Distribution Center in your state. (The local IRS office can give you the address of the Center.) You won't find all the objects you may be looking for, since the publication is intended for business depreciation, but you'll find many.

A method to estimate the total value of your possessions is to take the items costing originally $100 or more and calculate the "actual" cash value for them. (Do not include more than $500 each of jewelry, furs, securities, stamps, boats, trailers or off-road recreational vehicles such as golf carts, snowmobiles, minibikes, etc. Leave out anything over $100 for the total of all money, bullion, and rare coins.) When you have the total cash value for all the high ticket items, multiply that figure by 10 and you'll have a very rough estimate of the total value of your possessions.

APPRAISALS FOR COLLECTIONS •   If you have antiques or fine art in your home or apartment, you should be aware of their values. This will probably involve appraisal by a qualified appraiser. Such appraisers can usually be located through local antiques clubs and art galleries. Be sure the appraisal is given in writing. If the value of such objects brings the total value of personal possessions above the 50% level of house coverage, additional coverage will have to be obtained, usually by "scheduling" the items on the homeowners policy. That means that each item is described, its value is listed, and a separate premium is paid. The term for this extra coverage is "floater."

You will find with stamp and coin collections, however, that much less expensive insurance may be obtained through national stamp and coin clubs. However, the limitations on these policies may be more stringent in terms of security required than called for by a homeowners policy.

HIGH CRIME AREAS •   If you live in a high crime area and homeowners theft protection is not available through the usual insurance agents, you may have to apply to the Federal government for Federal Crime Insurance, a special program for residents of 22 states and the District of Columbia. Plans, however, are being drawn up for coverage in other states. If you are refused a homeowners policy because you live in a high crime area, this may be for you. While the limit is $10,000, and your house or apartment must be equipped with prescribed types of locks, the premium for $10,000 is comparatively modest, even in the highest crime areas. The coverage covers both burglary (where you are not physically involved) and robbery (where you are physically involved).

For information and application forms, write

Safety Management Institute
Federal Crime Insurance
P.O. Box 41033
Washington, DC 20014

HIGH FIRE RISK AREAS •   If you live in an area where you cannot get a regular homeowners policy because of high fire risk, you may qualify for FAIR (Fair Access to Insurance Requirements) coverage, set up by groups of insurance companies within certain states. The policies offer fire insurance and a special "extended coverage" endorsement which covers damage from

15

smoke, windstorm and hail, explosion, aircraft, vehicles, and riot. FAIR is currently offered in 26 states, Puerto Rico, and the District of Columbia, and plans are being drawn up for other states. If you are turned down for homeowners insurance because you live in a high fire risk area, contact your local insurance agent about FAIR.

FLOOD RISK COVERAGE • Homeowners policies do not cover against flood (see table), so if you live in a flood-prone area, and your communities have set up certain required flood control and land use programs, you can buy coverage on a house and personal property. These policies are issued through private insurance companies, but are subsidized by the government. Though you can also buy unsubsidized insurance, its premiums are usually extremely high. Check with your local agent to see if subsidized insurance is issued in your area.

EARTHQUAKE RISK • If you live in an area subject to earthquakes, you may find that the exclusion of that peril from your homeowners policy is unsettling. If so, you will be able to buy special coverage against loss from earthquake, usually through your local insurance agent who sold you the homeowners policy. But, be warned, the premiums are high.

SPECIAL PERIL EXCLUSIONS • In some areas, insurance companies exclude, by special rider, certain perils which are otherwise insured against in a homeowners policy. The most common of these is tornado, cyclone or hurricane loss. If you have such a rider, insurance is available as a special endorsement at extra cost from most companies.

You owe it to yourself to make sure you are covered against all risks to your property. One of the surest ways is to keep adequate insurance coverage on your home and personal possessions. Another is to keep this Register up to date with information on each of your possessions as you acquire them. And don't forget to delete those possessions which you sell or discard. When it comes time to make a claim for loss, this Register will be an inventory of your losses and will save you a great deal of time and trouble.

Table Of Homeowners Insurance

This information on coverage under homeowners insurance policies is general and for use as guidelines only. Each insurance company has variations from the standard form, and coverages may vary from state to state. (For example, some areas are able to buy policies where tornados, hurricanes, and cyclones are specifically excluded from coverage.) Ask your insurance agent about the coverage, exclusions, and limitations to policies available to you. Read the policy carefully before signing it. You can use the following lists of coverage and exclusions, limitations, and conditions to check against your policy. Where there are variations, your agent will be able to explain the differences and let you know what additional coverage is available for additional cost.

Perils Protected Against

a. Fire or Lightning

b. Removal of property from premises endangered by perils insured against. Covered for 30 days pro rata at each place moved to for preservation or repair

c.   Windstorm or Hail (see Exclusions 14 and 15)

d.   Explosion

e.   Riot or Civil Commotion, including pillage and looting

f.   Aircraft, including self-propelled missiles and spacecraft

g.   Vehicles

h.   Smoke of sudden and accidental nature (see Exclusion 16)

i.   Vandalism or Malicious Mischief (see Exclusion 11)

j.   Glass Damage

k.   Theft* (see Exclusions 17, 18, 19, 20, 21, and 22)

(Coverage under HO-1 Policies ends here)

l.   Falling Objects, but not loss to property inside a building unless exterior of roof or walls is damaged by the object

m.   Weight of Ice, Snow or Sleet, but only to property inside a building and only if the weight results in physical damage to the building

n.   Tearing asunder, cracking, burning, or bulging suddenly and accidentally of a steam or hot water heating system, but not including loss caused by or resulting from freezing

o.   Discharge, leakage or overflow of water or steam accidentally from a plumbing, heating or air conditioning system or domestic appliance, but not loss to the appliance involved (see Exclusion 12)

p.   Freezing of plumbing, heating or air conditioning systems, and domestic appliances (see Exclusion 3)

q.   Sudden and accidental injury to electrical appliances, devices, fixtures, and wiring from electrical currents artificially generated, except to tubes, transistors, and similar electrical components

---

*A Customer Safekeeping Policy can be purchased to cover any valuables or coins of numismatic value contained in any bank vault, bank safe deposit box, etc. Money is *not* covered. All items kept in the box should be appraised. DO NOT keep the appraisal in the safe deposit or vault with the valuables.

Exclusions To Coverage

1. Damage or loss caused by, resulting from, contributed to or aggravated by:
   a. Flood, Surface Water, Waves, Tidal Water or Tidal Waves, Overflow of Streams or other bodies of water, or spray from any of these, whether driven by wind or not;
   b. Water which backs up through sewers or drains;
   c. Water below the surface of the ground, including that which exerts pressure on or flows, seeps or leaks through sidewalks, driveways, foundations, walls, basement or other floors or through doors, windows or any other openings in such sidewalks, driveways, foundations, walls or floors;
   unless loss by fire or explosion is caused by the above, and then only for such loss by fire or explosion. Exclusions do not apply to loss by theft resulting from the above perils.

2. Damage or loss caused by, resulting from, contributed to or aggravated by: Earthquake, Volcanic Eruption, Landslide, Mudflow, Earth Sinking, Rising or Shifting or any Earth Movement, except for loss by fire, explosion or glass breakage and then only for such loss by fire, explosion or glass breakage. Exclusions do not apply to loss by theft resulting from earth movement perils;

3. Loss or damage to plumbing, heating or air conditioning systems or domestic appliances, or by discharge, leakage or overflow caused by or resulting from freezing while the building covered is vacant or unoccupied unless the insured shall have exercised due diligence in maintaining heat in the building or unless such systems and appliances had been drained and the water supply shut off during such vacancy or unoccupancy;

4. Loss or damage caused directly or indirectly by local or state law regulating construction, repair or demolition of buildings or structures, unless such peril is specifically endorsed on the policy;

5. Damage or loss to fences, pavements, patios, swimming pools, foundations, retaining walls, bulkheads, piers, wharves or docks caused by Freezing, Thawing or by the pressure or weight of ice or water whether driven by wind or not;

6. Damage or loss caused by or resulting from Power, Heating or Cooling Failure, unless failure is caused by physical damage to power, heating or cooling equipment on the premises caused by a covered peril;

7. Damage or loss caused by nuclear reaction or nuclear radiation or radioactive contamination, controlled or uncontrolled. Nuclear reaction or radiation or radioactive contamination is not "explosion" or "smoke";

8. Any secondary or seasonal residence, including property contained therein, wholly or jointly owned by an insured (however, a secondary residence endorsement may be added to the policy for an additional premium);

9. (Applying to coverage for house, detached structures and additional living expenses resulting from such loss)
   a. Loss or damage by Wear and Tear, Marring or Scratching, Deterioration, Inherent Vice, Latent

Defect, Mechanical Breakdown, Rust, Mold, Wet or Dry Rot, Contamination, Smog, Smoke from agricultural smudging or industrial operations, Settling, Cracking, Shrinkage, Bulging or Expansion of pavements, patios, foundations, walls, floors, roofs or ceilings.

b.   Birds, Vermin, Rodents, Insects or Domestic Animals; unless loss by fire, smoke (other than from agricultural smudging or industrial operations), explosion, collapse of a building, glass breakage by water not otherwise excluded ensues, the policy will cover only such ensuing loss. If loss by water not otherwise excluded ensues, the policy will also cover the cost of tearing out and replacing of any part of the building covered required to effect repairs to the plumbing, heating or air conditioning system or domestic appliance by excluding loss to the system or appliance from which the water escapes;

10.   Loss or damage by theft in or to a building under construction or of materials or supplies for it until the dwelling is completed and occupied;

11.   Loss or damage by vandalism and malicious mischief or glass breakage, if the property covered had been vacant beyond a period of 30 consecutive days immediately before the loss;

12.   Loss caused by continuous or repeated seepage or leakage of water or steam from within a plumbing, heating or air conditioning system or from within a domestic appliance which occurs over a period of weeks, months or years;

13.   Loss or damage caused directly or indirectly by frost or cold weather or ice (other than hail), snow or sleet, all whether driven by wind or not;

14.   Loss or damage caused by rain, snow, sand or dust, all whether driven by wind or not, unless the building containing the property covered first sustains an actual damage to roof or walls by the direct force of wind or hail and then the company will be liable for loss to the property covered which is caused by rain, snow, sand or dust entering the building through openings in the roof or walls made by direct action of wind or hail;

15.   Loss or damage by windstorm or hail to watercraft (except rowboats and canoes on premises) including their trailers, furnishings, equipment, and outboard motors while such property is not inside fully enclosed buildings;

16.   Loss or damage from smoke from agricultural smudging or industrial operations;

17.   Theft if committed by the insured;

18.   Theft of a precious or semi-precious stone from its setting;

19.   Theft of any device or instrument designed for recording or reproducing sound, and any tape, wire, record disc or other medium for use with such devices, from any automobile, watercraft or recreational vehicle;

20.   Theft of Snowmobiles, Golf carts, Land Rovers, Amphicars, Minibikes, Hill Scooters, Dune Buggies and other similar recreational motorized vehicles not licensed for road use, including their trailers (whether licensed or not), furnishings, and equipment;

21.   Theft from the insured dwelling while the portion customarily occupied exclusively by the insured is rented to others:

a.   of money, bullion, numismatic property or bank notes;

b.   of securities, accounts, bills, deeds, evidences of debt, letters of credit, notes other than bank notes, passports, railroad and other tickets or stamps, including philatelic property;

c.   of jewelry, watches, necklaces, bracelets, gems, precious and semi-precious stones, articles of gold and platinum, or furs;

d.   caused by a tenant, his employees or members of his household;

22.   Theft of property away from the insured premises:

a.   property while in any dwelling or premises owned, rented or occupied by the insured, except while the insured is temporarily residing there;

b.   property while unattended in or on any motor vehicle or trailer, other than a public conveyance, unless the loss is the result of forcible entry into the vehicle while all doors, windows or other openings are closed and locked, provided there are visible marks of forcible entry upon the exterior of the vehicle, or the loss is the result of the theft of the vehicle which is not recovered within 30 days; but property shall not be considered unattended when the insured is required to surrender the keys of the vehicle to a bailee (such as the attendant at a parking garage);

c.   property while unattended in or upon private watercraft unless the loss is the direct result of forcible entry into a securely locked compartment and provided there are visible marks of forcible entry upon the exterior of such compartment;

d.   watercraft, their furnishings, equipment and outboard motors;

e.   trailers, whether licensed or not.

Limits To Coverage

a.   Coverage will include loss to trees, shrubs, plants and lawns (except those grown for business purposes) only when the loss is caused by fire, lightning, explosion, riot, civil commotion, vandalism, malicious mischief, theft, aircraft, or vehicles not owned or operated by an occupant of the premises. Reimbursement for loss in any one occurrence will not be more than (in the aggregate for all such property) 5% of the limit of liability for coverage of the house (or 10% of the coverage of personal property for HO-4 and HO-6 policies) and not more than $250 for any one tree, shrub or plant, including the expense incurred for removing its debris.

b.   Under coverage for unscheduled personal property, the policy will not pay more for any one occurrence than:

i. $100 in the aggregate on money, bullion, numismatic property, and bank notes;

ii. $500 in the aggregate on securities, accounts, bills, deeds, evidences of debt, letters of credit, notes other than bank notes, passports, railroad and other tickets or stamps, including philatelic property;

iii. $500 in the aggregate on watercraft, including their trailers (whether licensed or not), furnishings, equipment, and outboard motors;

iv. $500 in the aggregate on snowmobiles, golf carts, land rovers, amphicars, minibikes, hill scooters, dune buggies, and other similar recreational motorized vehicles not licensed for road use including their trailers (whether licensed or not), furnishings, and equipment; coverage will be afforded only if such vehicles are on the insured premises and in a fully enclosed building;

v. $500 on trailers not otherwise provided for in iii or iv above, whether licensed or not;

vi. $1,000 in the aggregate for loss by theft of jewelry, watches, necklaces, bracelets, gems, precious and semi-precious stones, gold, platinum, and furs;

vii. $1,000 in the aggregate on all personal property, not otherwise excluded, which is lost, damaged or destroyed by theft or attempted theft while located in a locked vehicle away from the described premises;

viii. $1,000 on manuscripts.

Conditions ⚜

A. REPLACEMENT COST FOR HOUSE AND OTHER STRUCTURES

This is applicable only to a building structure covered, excluding outdoor radio and television antennas and aerials, carpeting, awnings, domestic appliances, outdoor equipment, cesspools and septic tanks, all whether attached to the building structure or not. *(Get a rider to cover this.)*

1. If, at the time of loss, the whole amount of insurance on the building for the peril causing the loss is 80% or more of the full replacement cost of such building, the coverage will be extended to include the full cost of repair or replacement (however, see a. below) without deduction for depreciation, for the part damaged or destroyed.

2. If, at the time of loss, the coverage is less than 80% of the full replacement value of the building, the reimbursement will not exceed the actual cash value of that part of the building damaged or destroyed.

3. The reimbursement will not exceed the smallest of the following amounts:

a. The face value of the policy;

b. The replacement cost of the building or any part of it intended for the same occupancy and use;

c. The amount actually and necessarily expended in repairing or replacing the building or any part of it intended for the same occupancy and use.

4. When the full cost of repair or replacement is more than $1,000 or more than 5% of the whole amount of insurance coverage, the company will not pay for any loss under 1 above unless and until actual repair or replacement is completed.

5. In determining whether the amount of insurance coverage is 80% or more of the full replacement value, the cost of excavations, underground flues and pipes, underground wiring and drains, and brick, stone and concrete foundations, piers and other supports which are below the under surface of the lowest basement floor or, where there is no basement, which are below the surface of the ground inside the foundation walls, shall be disregarded.

6. The insured may disregard this condition in making his claim, but such election will not prejudice his right to make further claim within 180 days after loss for any additional liability brought about by this policy condition.

B. LOSS CLAUSE •
Loss experienced will not reduce the amount of coverage that the policy offers in the future.

C. MORTGAGE CLAUSE (on coverage for house and other structures only) •
This only applies if the name of a mortgage holder is entered on the policy (as required by most mortgage organizations).

1. Reimbursement of loss under the policy will be paid to mortgage holders in the order of precedence, and shall not be invalidated by sale, foreclosure, or failure of the owner to pay the premium, if the mortgage holder will pay the premium if requested by the insurance company;

2. Mortgage holder must notify the insurance company of any change in ownership or occupancy or increase in hazard known to the mortgage holder;

3. If the insurance company cancels the policy, it will remain in force for the mortgage holder for 10 days after notification of the mortgage holder;

4. If the insurance company pays for loss or damage to the mortgage holder, the owner must look to the mortgage holder for recovery of the amount.

D. PERMISSION IS GRANTED BY THE INSURANCE COMPANY

1. for usual use of the building as a dwelling;

2. for the premises to be vacant without any time limit, except as it affects certain perils; (A building under construction will not be considered vacant.)

3. for the insured to make alterations, additions and repairs;

4. for the insured to make temporary repairs or permanent repairs after loss under the policy, intended to keep the property from further loss or damage. The policy requires that the insured must take steps to protect the property from further damage. Cost of such repairs must be recorded, and if they are directly attributable to damage by any peril covered, will be included in determining the amount of loss.

E. OTHER INSURANCE •
1. No other insurance is permitted to cover the building, except for perils not covered by the homeowners policy.

2. If there is insurance on certain personal property, the coverage under the homeowners policy will only be paid if the other insurance policy does not completely cover the loss.

F. NUCLEAR CLAUSE •
A nuclear reaction, nuclear radiation or radioactive contamination and any loss from those sources are not covered by the homeowners policy. However, direct loss by fire resulting from nuclear causes is insured against.

G. OCCUPANCY CLAUSE •
The homeowners policy will not cover a farm building or dwelling, unless the agricultural products produced on the farm are incidental to the occupancy of the dwelling and are principally for home consumption, or the buildings are in addition to a complete set of farm buildings and are not nearer than 200 feet to the farm buildings, and the occupants of the insured dwelling are not engaged in the operation of the farm.

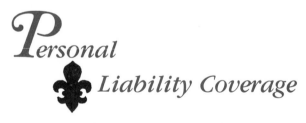

Personal Liability Coverage

The world today is becoming more conscious of legal liabilities and the opportunity to sue for legal redress. Where a few years ago a neighbor tripping on a root in your garden would grin embarrassedly and limp away, today that same neighbor might sue you for several thousands of dollars for injury and "pain and suffering."

Personal liability insurance, therefore, is a major form of protection, particularly for the home owner, but for the apartment dweller, as well. Homeowners insurance policies carry a standard personal liability coverage of $25,000. But today, that is often woefully inadequate. Such coverage may, through a rider, be increased to a larger amount, say $100,000, but even that is considered far too low by many insurance specialists.

The solution for the average homeowner is a special policy called "umbrella" coverage. It's really very simple. It's like "major medical" insurance, which covers you for crisis situations when your regular medical insurance isn't enough. The cost is very low for this "extra" coverage.

It's a liability policy for coverage of $1,000,000 or higher. It only covers you, however, for any judgment which might be levied against you in excess of the insurance you regularly carry for personal liability. Most policies do not cover for liability below $25,000 although some insurance companies will write them for lower amounts.

Say you have raised your homeowners policy to $100,000 personal liability coverage and have purchased an umbrella policy for $1,000,000 coverage. A friend, over to swim in your pool, slips on the diving board, and breaks his back. He sues you for $2,000,000.

The case is settled out of court for only $200,000. Your homeowners policy pays the first $100,000 — the limit of their liability — and your umbrella policy pays the remaining $100,000. If you didn't have the umbrella policy, that second $100,000 would have to come out of your savings, or a garnishment against your salary might be made if you didn't have the savings or assets to cover the judgment.

However, it is better to have high limits of umbrella coverage to avoid another problem. In the example of the friend who broke his back at your pool, he sued for $2,000,000. Even with a coverage of $1,000,000, you would be faced with expensive lawyer's fees. Your insurance company would defend you only to the limit of the $1,000,000. You would be forced to hire a lawyer to defend you against the other $1,000,000 of the claim. A coverage of $2,000,000 would have saved you the expense of hiring your own attorney.

Such high coverage is almost a necessity for anyone driving a car. Recent court decisions have awarded up to $2,000,000 for damages to a carfull of people injured by another driver.

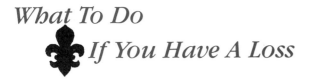

What To Do
If You Have A Loss

If you are subjected to a loss from burglary or natural perils, there are a number of steps which you should follow to make the procedure of recovery as painless as possible:

1. In case of vandalism or burglary, notify the police authorities as quickly as possible. (Notice should be made the moment you discover the damage or loss.)

2. In case of flooding, backup of sewage, etc., notify your local health department. There are health hazards in such conditions, and you may avoid danger to you and your family if prompt notification is made.

3. Notify your insurance agent. Your agent will inform you of the procedure for claiming the loss against your insurance, and will provide you with the proper forms for submission of your claim.

4. Itemize your precise loss. This will be necessary for the police in cases of vandalism and burglary and for the insurance company in any case. Here, this book will be your greatest asset, since you will have a listing of all of the major possessions in the proper form to make a report. (By checking against the listing in this Register, you will be able to quickly inventory your possessions, room by room, to determine exactly what has been lost or damaged.)

In addition to these steps, there are several others which apply to specific types of recovery:

Burglary

If you have been burglarized, it is essential that you disturb as little as possible before the police arrive on the scene. They may wish to take fingerprints, particularly around the area of entry.

If your police department does not take fingerprints, do not think it is because they are not interested in catching the criminals and recovering your property. Despite detective stories, movies and TV, police have found that finding usable fingerprints only occurs in a minority of cases. Professional burglars usually wear gloves, while juvenile offenders — who are the main cause of home burglaries — seldom have fingerprints on record. (Police also report that many householders complain bitterly about the difficulty of cleaning up fingerprint powder, which contains very fine aluminum and is hard to remove.)

1.   Notify the police if you have properly marked your major possessions, such as radios, TV, cameras, stereo, etc., with identification numbers. This will permit them to inform shopkeepers who might be offered the stolen items.

2.   Give the police a complete inventory of your missing possessions. They will want a preliminary inventory when they arrive to investigate, and will wish a complete inventory with model and serial numbers as soon as you can prepare it.

Fire

If you have had a fire, it may be impossible to inventory your loss immediately after the occurrence. However, if the loss was not total, it is vital that you protect your remaining possessions.

1.   If the house or apartment is not habitable, request the police for protection of the premises, to prevent loss by looting. (It is amazing how many neighbors — in any kind of neighborhood — will consider it perfectly ethical to take something they fancy, with the off-hand justification, "Oh well, the insurance will pay for that, anyway.")

a.   Police may put a guard on the house overnight to give you an opportunity to get help to remove undamaged possessions, or to board up the doors and windows to prevent entry.
b.   In an apartment, the door should be securely fastened and any windows opening on a fire escape should be boarded up to prevent break-in if the apartment is uninhabitable after the fire.

If the dwelling is habitable, attempt to close the burned area off from the rest of the building. Since there is smoke damage from fire — which includes the odor clinging to drapes, rugs, upholstered furniture, beds, clothing, etc. — be sure you have inventoried all of those items which have been damaged by either smoke deposit or odor. It is also a good idea to have a carpet cleaning firm and a drape cleaning firm make estimates on how much it will cost to remove smoke stains and odor from these items. Based on recent dry cleaning bills, estimate how much cleaning cost will be involved in removing stain and odor from clothing and other items which may be dry cleaned. (Most insurance companies balk at paying for removing odor by laundering if you live in a dwelling with a washing machine.) Attach the estimates of restoring various items stained or damaged by smoke odor. If you are told that some items cannot be renewed, this is the basis for claiming loss on those items to the insurance company.

If you have provided an estimate for cleaning, and the insurance company pays on that basis, but the cleaning is unsuccessful, you can make a claim for total loss. However, most insurance firms will then subtract the cost of cleaning from the amount reimbursed for the loss.

Flood or Sewage Backup

If you live in an area subject to flood, hopefully you will have obtained Federal flood insurance. Flood, sewage backup, and basement flooding are not protected by a homeowners insurance policy. If you have loss or damage from any of these perils and you are not covered by insurance, there are a number of things you can do to minimize destruction.

If upholstered furniture has been soaked, immediately contact a furniture cleaning service. It is vital that you make the contact before the upholstery dries. In many cases of flooding, the upholstery can be cleaned and dried without any great damage. Never place soaked furniture in the sun to dry; it will cause wood to warp and the finish to fade and check.

If you have had books or valuable papers soaked, preserve them by freezing as quickly as possible. While you are seeking a service which can properly dry these documents or books by freeze drying (the latest method of treating valuable books and papers which have been soaked) the freezing will prevent further deterioration of the items.

All objects which have been soaked should be separated for drying. This means that clothing should be hung on hangers to dry evenly; all items should be removed from the tops of tables, dressers, chests, etc., and all drawers of dressers and chests should be emptied.

Experts disagree on whether drawers should be removed from dressers or desks during drying. Contact your local furniture dealer and ask his or her opinion. In any case, if drawers are left in a dresser or desk, they should be pulled out enough (probably two to three inches) to permit the interior of the piece to dry quickly.

Windstorm

If your roof has been damaged, or windows broken by windstorm, one of the first things you should do is protect the possessions inside your house. Often wind is accompanied or followed by rain or snow. If a window is broken, it should be covered from the outside by a sheet of plywood or sheet plastic held down by strips of wood around the edges of the window frame. If part of the roof has been removed, remove all items from the attic, and — if possible — attempt to cover the opening in the roof with either plastic (held down by strips of wood nailed into the roof) or a tarpaulin held down the same way. If this is impossible, sheet plastic or a tarpaulin should be spread over the ceiling below the opening to prevent rain or snow from leaking through into the rooms below.

If you are in a tornado or hurricane area, you will have to have special insurance to cover these perils, since homeowners policies generally have a rider excluding such perils in an area prone to these occurrences. In other sections of the country, windstorm is covered by homeowners insurance.

As with any other loss, be sure to inventory all lost items or damage. Get an estimate for permanent repair of the roof or window, but do not fail to make temporary repairs to prevent further damage. (Insurance policies will not cover loss caused because homeowners were not diligent in protecting their property from further damage.)

Homeowners insurance generally will reimburse for the cost of temporary repairs to protect the contents of a house. In most cases, it will also provide reimbursement for repairs required to protect contents of an apartment or condominium, but not permanent repairs — which are covered in the overall building policy.

Windstorm frequently causes damage and destruction to trees and shrubs. Any such damage is covered in most homeowners policies. If you have such damage, remember that there is a $250 limit (in most policies) on any one tree or shrub, and that the costs of removing debris are considered part of the reimbursement. It often makes sense economically to borrow or rent a chain saw and cut up and remove a downed tree yourself, rather than to call in a tree service to perform the task.

If you have problems collecting a claim

Generally, insurance companies writing homeowners policies pay claims promptly. However, there are sometimes escape clauses in the policies which permit them to delay payment. In some cases, this could cause great inconvenience.

If you have such a problem, and get no satisfaction from the local agent, contact the insurance company head office. The city and state of the home office is generally given on the policy form. Write to or phone the "policyholder service department." The name may vary from company to company, but all casualty firms have such a department.

Normally you should be able to resolve your difficulties by communicating with the head office. However, when all else has failed, and only as a last resort, you can lodge a complaint with the State Insurance Commissioner.

*T*ax Considerations

There are a number of tax considerations to be made in connection with personal possessions. Some sales of property have serious tax consequences. Some repairs or improvements to property often have major tax effect. And there are tax considerations in the loss of property.

Selling Your Home

The sale of your home (house, condominium, cooperative) may have serious tax consequences. In order to minimize the tax impact of such a sale, it is advisable to maintain careful records of all transactions affecting the cost of your home — from its purchase through all additions and improvements — shrubbery, insulation, siding, shelving, appliances, plumbing, etc. (See list)

Some improvements, such as insulation, storm doors, solar heating, and other energy saving devices, may entitle you to an energy tax credit. Reflecting these improvements in your book serves as a reminder to your tax preparer.

If you are in doubt as to what constitutes an improvement (as opposed to "repair" or "maintenance," which are not eligible for tax consideration) record it anyway. Let your tax advisor eliminate it when he is assembling your information.

You will be amazed at how much money you will spend on additions and improvements, whether you own a home, a condominium or a cooperative apartment. Without realizing it, these sums build up to increase the tax "base" or cost of your home, and therefore reduce your ultimate taxable gain when you sell.

Loss or Damage

In the event of theft, vandalism, fire or other casualty, there is a tax deduction if the loss is not reimbursed fully by insurance. Your possessions record will help you establish and support casualty loss claims.

Some casualty losses are not covered by ordinary homeowners insurance. While it may be possible to buy additional coverage for these perils through endorsements to a homeowners policy, or through special Federal or Federally-subsidized insurance, many homeowners fall prey to perils for which they have not obtained insurance. These perils include flood, earthquake, sewers backing up, mudslide, land sinking, etc. In some parts of the country, homeowners insurance does not include tornados, cyclones or hurricanes.

If you find yourself in these situations, you may take some comfort in the knowledge that at your next income tax filing, the Internal Revenue Service will permit you to deduct those casualty losses from your income tax. However, there is a $100 deductible on casualty losses reported on your tax return. It applies to each individual incident. In other words, if you had a storm cause flooding of your basement, unreimbursed by insurance, when you report the $750 loss and damage which resulted, you will have to deduct $100 from the amount reported. If you later had an earthquake, also uninsured, you would have to deduct $100 from that loss also when you report it on your tax.

Even more common is the deductible on your homeowners policy itself. Often policies are purchased with deductibles as high as $250 per loss. This substantially reduces the cost of the insurance, but it reduces payment for loss by that much. Loss caused by an insurance deductible is also deductible from your income at tax time, although that too will be subject to the $100 loss deduction on the tax return.

Finally, some losses are limited under the homeowners policy. For example, furs are only covered against burglary up to the amount of $250. If you had a $1,500 fur coat stolen from your apartment, you would receive only $250 from the insurance company. The remaining $1,250, however, could be deducted from your income tax return, subject, of course, to the $100 deductible.

Looking Ahead

Executors of your estate will also find your possessions register an indispensable tool in settling your estate with state and Federal tax authorities.

If you are tax conscious (and who isn't) use this book to its fullest extent and keep it up-to-date. By bringing up to date all entries about purchases, disposition, loss or improvements (to house, condominium or cooperative apartment) to your property at least once a year — Federal income tax preparation time is ideal — you will have a current record. You'll be surprised how much money and how many headaches it will save you.

Examples of improvements and additions which increase the tax base of your home:

Construction of a playroom in your basement
Adding a workshop to your garage
Adding a bathroom to the house
Paving a driveway
Insulating walls, ceilings, floors (eligible for existing energy tax credits)
Adding a swimming pool
Adding a terrace
Constructing retaining walls
Constructing a new porch or deck
Installing:
   Storm windows and doors (eligible for existing energy tax credits)
   Humidifier in heating system
   Air conditioning (window, through the wall or central unit)
   Shrubbery and landscaping
   Appliances (stove, refrigerator, washer, drier, garbage disposal, compactor, dishwasher)
   Siding
   Elevator
   Built-in vacuum system
   Permanent sump pump
   Attic fan
   Ceiling fans

Electric fixtures
New kitchen cabinets
Built-ins (cabinets, bookcases)
New floors
    Tiles
    Wood
    Wall-to-wall carpeting
New wiring and outlets
Sewer lines, cesspool, septic tank
Well, water pump
New boiler or furnace
New hot water heater (solar heaters are eligible for existing energy tax credits)
Replacing fuse boxes by circuit breakers
Replacing roof

Warranties
And What They Mean

      The average person does not read the warranty which comes with a new possession. Yet, if anything goes wrong, that warranty — if any — is the only legal recourse available. To most people, the reputation for fairness and reliability of the dealer or shopkeeper is the best warranty. However, today, with ever more complex devices used in the home — and on the road — the seller is often not equipped to do repairs or make replacements of expensive items.

      Read your warranties carefully. Under a law called the Magnuson-Moss Warranty Act, *if* a manufacturer gives you a warranty, it must be clearly one of two types: a full warranty or a limited warranty. And you must be allowed to see the warranty for any item which costs $15 or more before you purchase it.

Full Warranty

      Under the Magnuson-Moss Act, a full warranty must guarantee that the manufacturer (or importer if the item is made out of the country) will:

    1.   Provide the warranty for anyone who owns the product during the warranty period. (That means that if you bought the item from the original owner and the warranty period is still in force, you can get service under the warranty conditions.)

    2.   Fix or replace a defective product, including removal and reinstallation if necessary, in a reasonable period of time. (Reasonable is not spelled out in the Act, but several months might be considered unreasonable.)

    3.   Not require you to do anything unreasonable, such as ship a mattress back to the factory in order to get warranty service. (However, smaller items might have to be taken to a repair station and picked up again, in order to get warranty service.)

    4.   Protect you from a "lemon." Although a full warranty may not have a lemon clause written into it, the M-M Act requires that if the product can't be fixed or hasn't been after a reasonable number of attempts, you get your choice of a new product or your money back. (The problem: The Act doesn't say what is a reasonable number of attempts.)

      One thing to watch out for. You may get a full warranty on one part of the item (such as a compressor in a refrigerator or an air conditioner, which has a full warranty for a five year period) and only a limited warranty for the rest of the product. Read the warranty carefully to determine just how well you are covered in case of a deficient product!

Limited Warranty

With a limited warranty, you get less protection. In other words, although the period of time may run the same as a full warranty (and there is nothing in the Act which imposes any length of time on a warranty; it may run 30 days to "lifetime") the coverage is limited.

Here are some typical limitations in a limited warranty:

— The warranty is restricted to the original owner.

— You get only a proportionate (pro rata) refund or credit on a trade-in, based upon the amount of time left in the warranty. (This is typical with automobile batteries. If you own a 4-year warranty battery which cost $50 for two years, you will get a refund or trade-in credit of $25.)

— You are only paid for parts to repair your defective product; you have to pay for the labor — usually the larger cost — yourself.

— You have to return the product for servicing or pay to have it shipped back to the factory.

— The warranty is restricted to "defects in materials or workmanship." (This means that products which simply "wear out" during the warranty period may not be covered unless there is a clearly detected "defect.")

Implied Warranties

What if you don't get a warranty with a new product you have just purchased? If it stops functioning or breaks within a few weeks, are you just out of luck? Not necessarily. There's such a thing in law as an "implied warranty."

In simple terms, this is really nothing else but the law's viewpoint that a product must be suitable for the use for which it is intended. A television set, for example, should provide both picture and sound.

However, to get satisfaction from an implied warranty, you often end up going to court. Sometimes the threat of going to court is enough to make the manufacturer settle on a defective product, since adverse publicity might restrict sales.

One warning: if you have purchased something labeled as "as is," you have no warranty of any type. You have purchased the product with the knowledge that there is no recourse, whether it works properly or not.

Where to Go for Help

If you really have a lemon, where do you go for help? (Say the dealer, and maybe the maker, have tried to fix it and have failed to correct it to your satisfaction.)

If you have an automobile, and have tried the dealer and the manufacturer (most of whom have regional service representatives for just this purpose), you have one other recourse before suing. It is the Automobile Consumer Action Panel (AUTOCAP). Finding one, however, isn't easy. Not all states have them (and they are set up by individual state automobile dealer groups). To locate the one in your state, call your local automobile dealers association.

If you have a major appliance (range, refrigerator, dishwasher, washing machine, etc.) you can turn to the Major Appliance Consumer Action Panel (MACAP), 20 N. Wacker Drive, Chicago, IL 60606. Toll free number is (800) 621-0477.

If your problem is with furniture, there is also a Furniture Industry Consumer Action Panel (FICAP), P.O. Box 951, High Point, NC 27261.

The purpose of a consumer action panel is to serve as a third-party mediation service between you and the manufacturer of the problem product. You are not legally required to accept the decision of the consumer action panel, and if you wish you can sue the maker after an adverse panel decision.

However, you may wish to go to the local Better Business Bureau for relief. There is one disadvantage to this, however. If you take your warranty problem to a BBB for arbitration, they will require you to waive your right to go to court. This is referred to as "binding arbitration." Both you and the manufacturer must agree to allowing the BBB to act as a middleman.

If you do go to court, you can do it under the Magnuson-Moss Warranty Act if the product was made after July 4, 1975. The Act provides that if you win, the warrantor must pay your legal costs as well as comply with the warranty. If your product was made before that time, you will have to sue under local state law on warranties, which varies widely from state to state.

Records

Keep all of the warranties for the products you buy in one place. Keep a current listing of all products in this Register. Update this Register each time you purchase a product which costs $15 or more. (You can also use it to list items of any cost.)

If any product does not function the way it should, look up the warranty and follow the instructions given by the manufacturer. In most cases, having the warranty precludes any problem in getting satisfaction. If you do not have a warranty, having an exact record in this Register makes your case under an "implied" warranty much stronger.

THE REGISTER

• MAJOR APPLIANCES •

Refrigerators, Ranges (Stoves), Dishwashers, Disposals, Trash Compactors, Freezers, Microwave Ovens, Hot Water Heaters, Furnaces, Air Conditioners, Humidifiers, Dehumidifiers, etc.

Item _____ Make _____ Model No. _____

Serial No. _____ Date Acquired _____ Cost _____

Item _____ Make _____ Model No. _____

Serial No. _____ Date Acquired _____ Cost _____

Item _____ Make _____ Model No. _____

Serial No. _____ Date Acquired _____ Cost _____

Item _____ Make _____ Model No. _____

Serial No. _____ Date Acquired _____ Cost _____

Item _____ Make _____ Model No. _____

Serial No. _____ Date Acquired _____ Cost _____

Item _____ Make _____ Model No. _____

Serial No. _____ Date Acquired _____ Cost _____

Item _____ Make _____ Model No. _____

Serial No. _____ Date Acquired _____ Cost _____

Item _____ Make _____ Model No. _____

Serial No. _____ Date Acquired _____ Cost _____

Item _____ Make _____ Model No. _____

Serial No. _____ Date Acquired _____ Cost _____

Item _____ Make _____ Model No. _____

Serial No. _____ Date Acquired _____ Cost _____

Item _____ Make _____ Model No. _____

Serial No. _____ Date Acquired _____ Cost _____

Item _____ Make _____ Model No. _____

Serial No. _____ Date Acquired _____ Cost _____

Item _____ Make _____ Model No. _____

Serial No. _____ Date Acquired _____ Cost _____

Item _____ Make _____ Model No. _____

Serial No. _____ Date Acquired _____ Cost _____

Item _____ Make _____ Model No. _____

Serial No. _____ Date Acquired _____ Cost _____

Item _____ Make _____ Model No. _____

Serial No. _____ Date Acquired _____ Cost _____

Item _____ Make _____ Model No. _____

Serial No. _____ Date Acquired _____ Cost _____

Item _____ Make _____ Model No. _____

Serial No. _____ Date Acquired _____ Cost _____

Item _____ Make _____ Model No. _____

Serial No. _____ Date Acquired _____ Cost _____

Item _____ Make _____ Model No. _____

Serial No. _____ Date Acquired _____ Cost _____

Item _____ Make _____ Model No. _____

Serial No. _____ Date Acquired _____ Cost _____

Item _____ Make _____ Model No. _____

Serial No. _____ Date Acquired _____ Cost _____

Item _____ Make _____ Model No. _____

Serial No. _____ Date Acquired _____ Cost _____

Item _____ Make _____ Model No. _____

Serial No. _____ Date Acquired _____ Cost _____

Item _____ Make _____ Model No. _____

Serial No. _____ Date Acquired _____ Cost _____

Item _____ Make _____ Model No. _____

Serial No. _____ Date Acquired _____ Cost _____

Item _____ Make _____ Model No. _____

Serial No. _____ Date Acquired _____ Cost _____

Item _____ Make _____ Model No. _____

Serial No. _____ Date Acquired _____ Cost _____

Item _____ Make _____ Model No. _____

Serial No. _____ Date Acquired _____ Cost _____

• SMALL ELECTRICAL APPLIANCES •

Toasters, Coffeemakers, Mixers, Food Processors, Irons, Hair Dryers, Razors, Heaters, Fans, Electric Pencil
Sharpeners, Calculators, Adding Machines, etc.

Item _____ Make _____ Model No. _____

Serial No. _____ Date Acquired _____ Cost _____

Item _____ Make _____ Model No. _____

Serial No. _____ Date Acquired _____ Cost _____

Item _____ Make _____ Model No. _____

Serial No. _____ Date Acquired _____ Cost _____

Item _____ Make _____ Model No. _____

Serial No. _____ Date Acquired _____ Cost _____

Item _____ Make _____ Model No. _____

Serial No. _____ Date Acquired _____ Cost _____

Item _____ Make _____ Model No. _____

Serial No. _____ Date Acquired _____ Cost _____

Item _____ Make _____ Model No. _____

Serial No. _____ Date Acquired _____ Cost _____

Item _____ Make _____ Model No. _____

Serial No. _____ Date Acquired _____ Cost _____

Item _____ Make _____ Model No. _____

Serial No. _____ Date Acquired _____ Cost _____

Item _____ Make _____ Model No. _____

Serial No. _____ Date Acquired _____ Cost _____

Item _____ Make _____ Model No. _____

Serial No. _____ Date Acquired _____ Cost _____

Item _____ Make _____ Model No. _____

Serial No. _____ Date Acquired _____ Cost _____

Item _____ Make _____ Model No. _____

Serial No. _____ Date Acquired _____ Cost _____

Item _____ Make _____ Model No. _____

Serial No. _____ Date Acquired _____ Cost _____

Item _____ Make _____ Model No. _____

Serial No. _____ Date Acquired _____ Cost _____

Item _____ Make _____ Model No. _____

Serial No. _____ Date Acquired _____ Cost _____

Item _____ Make _____ Model No. _____

Serial No. _____ Date Acquired _____ Cost _____

Item _____ Make _____ Model No. _____

Serial No. _____ Date Acquired _____ Cost _____

Item _____ Make _____ Model No. _____

Serial No. _____ Date Acquired _____ Cost _____

Item _____ Make _____ Model No. _____

Serial No. _____ Date Acquired _____ Cost _____

Item _____ Make _____ Model No. _____

Serial No. _____ Date Acquired _____ Cost _____

Item _____ Make _____ Model No. _____

Serial No. _____ Date Acquired _____ Cost _____

Item _____ Make _____ Model No. _____

Serial No. _____ Date Acquired _____ Cost _____

Item _____ Make _____ Model No. _____

Serial No. _____ Date Acquired _____ Cost _____

Item _____ Make _____ Model No. _____

Serial No. _____ Date Acquired _____ Cost _____

Item _____ Make _____ Model No. _____

Serial No. _____ Date Acquired _____ Cost _____

Item _____ Make _____ Model No. _____

Serial No. _____ Date Acquired _____ Cost _____

Item _____ Make _____ Model No. _____

Serial No. _____ Date Acquired _____ Cost _____

Item _____ Make _____ Model No. _____

Serial No. _____ Date Acquired _____ Cost _____

Item _____ Make _____ Model No. _____

Serial No. _____ Date Acquired _____ Cost _____

Item _____ Make _____ Model No. _____

Serial No. _____ Date Acquired _____ Cost _____

Item _____ Make _____ Model No. _____

Serial No. _____ Date Acquired _____ Cost _____

Item _____ Make _____ Model No. _____

Serial No. _____ Date Acquired _____ Cost _____

Item _____ Make _____ Model No. _____

Serial No. _____ Date Acquired _____ Cost _____

Item _____ Make _____ Model No. _____

Serial No. _____ Date Acquired _____ Cost _____

Item _____ Make _____ Model No. _____

Serial No. _____ Date Acquired _____ Cost _____

Item _____ Make _____ Model No. _____

Serial No. _____ Date Acquired _____ Cost _____

Item _____ Make _____ Model No. _____

Serial No. _____ Date Acquired _____ Cost _____

• HOME ENTERTAINMENT EQUIPMENT •

Televisions, Radios, Stereos, Hi-Fis, Phonographs, Video Recorders, Video Games, Tape Recorders, Cassette Recorders, etc.

Item _____ Make _____ Model No. _____

Serial No. _____ Date Acquired _____ Cost _____

Item _____ Make _____ Model No. _____

Serial No. _____ Date Acquired _____ Cost _____

Item _____ Make _____ Model No. _____

Serial No. _____ Date Acquired _____ Cost _____

Item _____ Make _____ Model No. _____

Serial No. _____ Date Acquired _____ Cost _____

Item _____ Make _____ Model No. _____

Serial No. _____ Date Acquired _____ Cost _____

Item _____ Make _____ Model No. _____

Serial No. _____ Date Acquired _____ Cost _____

Item _____ Make _____ Model No. _____

Serial No. _____ Date Acquired _____ Cost _____

Item _____ Make _____ Model No. _____

Serial No. _____ Date Acquired _____ Cost _____

Item _____ Make _____ Model No. _____

Serial No. _____ Date Acquired _____ Cost _____

Item _____ Make _____ Model No. _____

Serial No. _____ Date Acquired _____ Cost _____

Item _____ Make _____ Model No. _____

Serial No. _____ Date Acquired _____ Cost _____

Item _____ Make _____ Model No. _____

Serial No. _____ Date Acquired _____ Cost _____

Item _____ Make _____ Model No. _____

Serial No. _____ Date Acquired _____ Cost _____

Item _____ Make _____ Model No. _____

Serial No. _____ Date Acquired _____ Cost _____

Item _____ Make _____ Model No. _____

Serial No. _____ Date Acquired _____ Cost _____

Item _____ Make _____ Model No. _____

Serial No. _____ Date Acquired _____ Cost _____

Item _____ Make _____ Model No. _____

Serial No. _____ Date Acquired _____ Cost _____

Item _____ Make _____ Model No. _____

Serial No. _____ Date Acquired _____ Cost _____

Item _____ Make _____ Model No. _____

Serial No. _____ Date Acquired _____ Cost _____

Item _____ Make _____ Model No. _____

Serial No. _____ Date Acquired _____ Cost _____

Item _____ Make _____ Model No. _____

Serial No. _____ Date Acquired _____ Cost _____

Item _____ Make _____ Model No. _____

Serial No. _____ Date Acquired _____ Cost _____

Item _____ Make _____ Model No. _____

Serial No. _____ Date Acquired _____ Cost _____

Item _____ Make _____ Model No. _____

Serial No. _____ Date Acquired _____ Cost _____

Item _____ Make _____ Model No. _____

Serial No. _____ Date Acquired _____ Cost _____

Item _____ Make _____ Model No. _____

Serial No. _____ Date Acquired _____ Cost _____

Item _____ Make _____ Model No. _____

Serial No. _____ Date Acquired _____ Cost _____

• PHOTOGRAPHIC EQUIPMENT •

Cameras, Lenses, Electronic Flash Units, Projectors, Enlargers, Timers, Exposure Meters, etc.

Item _____ Make _____ Model No. _____

Serial No. _____ Date Acquired _____ Cost _____

Item _____ Make _____ Model No. _____

Serial No. _____ Date Acquired _____ Cost _____

Item _____ Make _____ Model No. _____

Serial No. _____ Date Acquired _____ Cost _____

Item _____ Make _____ Model No. _____

Serial No. _____ Date Acquired _____ Cost _____

Item _____ Make _____ Model No. _____

Serial No. _____ Date Acquired _____ Cost _____

Item _____ Make _____ Model No. _____

Serial No. _____ Date Acquired _____ Cost _____

Item _____ Make _____ Model No. _____

Serial No. _____ Date Acquired _____ Cost _____

Item _____ Make _____ Model No. _____

Serial No. _____ Date Acquired _____ Cost _____

Item _____ Make _____ Model No. _____

Serial No. _____ Date Acquired _____ Cost _____

Item _____ Make _____ Model No. _____

Serial No. _____ Date Acquired _____ Cost _____

Item _____ Make _____ Model No. _____

Serial No. _____ Date Acquired _____ Cost _____

Item _____ Make _____ Model No. _____

Serial No. _____ Date Acquired _____ Cost _____

Item _____ Make _____ Model No. _____

Serial No. _____ Date Acquired _____ Cost _____

Item _____ Make _____ Model No. _____

Serial No. _____ Date Acquired _____ Cost _____

Item _____ Make _____ Model No. _____

Serial No. _____ Date Acquired _____ Cost _____

Item _____ Make _____ Model No. _____

Serial No. _____ Date Acquired _____ Cost _____

Item _____ Make _____ Model No. _____

Serial No. _____ Date Acquired _____ Cost _____

Item _____ Make _____ Model No. _____

Serial No. _____ Date Acquired _____ Cost _____

Item _____ Make _____ Model No. _____

Serial No. _____ Date Acquired _____ Cost _____

Item _____ Make _____ Model No. _____

Serial No. _____ Date Acquired _____ Cost _____

Item _____ Make _____ Model No. _____

Serial No. _____ Date Acquired _____ Cost _____

Item _____ Make _____ Model No. _____

Serial No. _____ Date Acquired _____ Cost _____

Item _____ Make _____ Model No. _____

Serial No. _____ Date Acquired _____ Cost _____

Item _____ Make _____ Model No. _____

Serial No. _____ Date Acquired _____ Cost _____

Item _____ Make _____ Model No. _____

Serial No. _____ Date Acquired _____ Cost _____

Item _____ Make _____ Model No. _____

Serial No. _____ Date Acquired _____ Cost _____

Item _____ Make _____ Model No. _____

Serial No. _____ Date Acquired _____ Cost _____

Item _____ Make _____ Model No. _____

Serial No. _____ Date Acquired _____ Cost _____

Item _____ Make _____ Model No. _____

Serial No. _____ Date Acquired _____ Cost _____

• POWERED TOOLS •

Circular Saws, Drills, Shapers, Routers, Saber Saws, Chain Saws, Sanders, Impact Tools, etc.

Item _____ Make _____ Model No. _____

Serial No. _____ Date Acquired _____ Cost _____

Item _____ Make _____ Model No. _____

Serial No. _____ Date Acquired _____ Cost _____

Item _____ Make _____ Model No. _____

Serial No. _____ Date Acquired _____ Cost _____

Item _____ Make _____ Model No. _____

Serial No. _____ Date Acquired _____ Cost _____

Item _____ Make _____ Model No. _____

Serial No. _____ Date Acquired _____ Cost _____

Item _____ Make _____ Model No. _____

Serial No. _____ Date Acquired _____ Cost _____

Item _____ Make _____ Model No. _____

Serial No. _____ Date Acquired _____ Cost _____

Item _____ Make _____ Model No. _____

Serial No. _____ Date Acquired _____ Cost _____

Item _____ Make _____ Model No. _____

Serial No. _____ Date Acquired _____ Cost _____

Item _____ Make _____ Model No. _____

Serial No. _____ Date Acquired _____ Cost _____

Item _____ Make _____ Model No. _____

Serial No. _____ Date Acquired _____ Cost _____

Item _____ Make _____ Model No. _____

Serial No. _____ Date Acquired _____ Cost _____

Item _____ Make _____ Model No. _____

Serial No. _____ Date Acquired _____ Cost _____

Item _____ Make _____ Model No. _____

Serial No. _____ Date Acquired _____ Cost _____

Item _____ Make _____ Model No. _____

Serial No. _____ Date Acquired _____ Cost _____

Item _____ Make _____ Model No. _____

Serial No. _____ Date Acquired _____ Cost _____

Item _____ Make _____ Model No. _____

Serial No. _____ Date Acquired _____ Cost _____

Item _____ Make _____ Model No. _____

Serial No. _____ Date Acquired _____ Cost _____

• HAND TOOLS •

Handsaws, Hammers, Chisels, Vises, Braces, Bits, Screwdrivers, Wrenches, etc.

Item _____ Size _____ Make _____

Date Acquired _____ Cost _____

Item _____ Size _____ Make _____

Date Acquired _____ Cost _____

Item _____ Size _____ Make _____

Date Acquired _____ Cost _____

Item _____ Size _____ Make _____

Date Acquired _____ Cost _____

Item _____ Size _____ Make _____

Date Acquired _____ Cost _____

Item _____ Size _____ Make _____

Date Acquired _____ Cost _____

Item _____ Size _____ Make _____

Date Acquired _____ Cost _____

Item _____ Size _____ Make _____

Date Acquired _____ Cost _____

Item _____ Size _____ Make _____

Date Acquired _____ Cost _____

Item _____ Size _____ Make _____

Date Acquired _____ Cost _____

Item _____ Size _____ Make _____

Date Acquired _____ Cost _____

Item _____ Size _____ Make _____

Date Acquired _____ Cost _____

Item _____ Size _____ Make _____

Date Acquired _____ Cost _____

Item _____ Size _____ Make _____

Date Acquired _____ Cost _____

Item _____ Size _____ Make _____

Date Acquired _____ Cost _____

Item _____ Size _____ Make _____

Date Acquired _____ Cost _____

Item _____ Size _____ Make _____

Date Acquired _____ Cost _____

Item _____ Size _____ Make _____

Date Acquired _____ Cost _____

Item _____ Size _____ Make _____

Date Acquired _____ Cost _____

Item _____ Size _____ Make _____

Date Acquired _____ Cost _____

Item _____ Size _____ Make _____

Date Acquired _____ Cost _____

Item _____ Size _____ Make _____

Date Acquired _____ Cost _____

Item _____ Size _____ Make _____

Date Acquired _____ Cost _____

Item _____ Size _____ Make _____

Date Acquired _____ Cost _____

Item _____ Size _____ Make _____

Date Acquired _____ Cost _____

Item _____ Size _____ Make _____

Date Acquired _____ Cost _____

Item _____ Size _____ Make _____

Date Acquired _____ Cost _____

Item _____ Size _____ Make _____

Date Acquired _____ Cost _____

Item _____ Size _____ Make _____

Date Acquired _____ Cost _____

Item _____ Size _____ Make _____

Date Acquired _____ Cost _____

• POWERED GARDEN EQUIPMENT •

Lawn Mowers, Trimmers, Sweepers, Snow Blowers, Leaf Blowers, Tillers, Tractors, Accessories, etc.

Item _____ Make _____ Model No. _____

Serial No. _____ Date Acquired _____ Cost _____

Item _____ Make _____ Model No. _____

Serial No. _____ Date Acquired _____ Cost _____

Item _____ Make _____ Model No. _____

Serial No. _____ Date Acquired _____ Cost _____

Item _____ Make _____ Model No. _____

Serial No. _____ Date Acquired _____ Cost _____

Item _____ Make _____ Model No. _____

Serial No. _____ Date Acquired _____ Cost _____

Item _____ Make _____ Model No. _____

Serial No. _____ Date Acquired _____ Cost _____

Item _____ Make _____ Model No. _____

Serial No. _____ Date Acquired _____ Cost _____

Item _____ Make _____ Model No. _____

Serial No. _____ Date Acquired _____ Cost _____

Item _____ Make _____ Model No. _____

Serial No. _____ Date Acquired _____ Cost _____

Item _____ Make _____ Model No. _____

Serial No. _____ Date Acquired _____ Cost _____

Item _____ Make _____ Model No. _____

Serial No. _____ Date Acquired _____ Cost _____

Item _____ Make _____ Model No. _____

Serial No. _____ Date Acquired _____ Cost _____

Item _____ Make _____ Model No. _____

Serial No. _____ Date Acquired _____ Cost _____

Item _____ Make _____ Model No. _____

Serial No. _____ Date Acquired _____ Cost _____

Item _____ Make _____ Model No. _____

Serial No. _____ Date Acquired _____ Cost _____

Item _____ Make _____ Model No. _____

Serial No. _____ Date Acquired _____ Cost _____

Item _____ Make _____ Model No. _____

Serial No. _____ Date Acquired _____ Cost _____

Item _____ Make _____ Model No. _____

Serial No. _____ Date Acquired _____ Cost _____

Item _____ Make _____ Model No. _____

Serial No. _____ Date Acquired _____ Cost _____

• HAND GARDEN TOOLS •

Shovels, Tree Saws, Hoes, Picks, Wheelbarrows, Carts, Rakes, Axes, Post Hole Diggers, Pool Tools, etc.

Item _____ Size _____ Make _____

Date Acquired _____ Cost _____

Item _____ Size _____ Make _____

Date Acquired _____ Cost _____

Item _____ Size _____ Make _____

Date Acquired _____ Cost _____

Item _____ Size _____ Make _____

Date Acquired _____ Cost _____

Item _____ Size _____ Make _____

Date Acquired _____ Cost _____

Item _____ Size _____ Make _____

Date Acquired _____ Cost _____

Item _____ Size _____ Make _____

Date Acquired _____ Cost _____

Item _____ Size _____ Make _____

Date Acquired _____ Cost _____

Item _____ Size _____ Make _____

Date Acquired _____ Cost _____

Item _____ Size _____ Make _____

Date Acquired _____ Cost _____

Item _____ Size _____ Make _____

Date Acquired _____ Cost _____

Item _____ Size _____ Make _____

Date Acquired _____ Cost _____

Item _____ Size _____ Make _____

Date Acquired _____ Cost _____

Item _____ Size _____ Make _____

Date Acquired _____ Cost _____

Item _____ Size _____ Make _____

Date Acquired _____ Cost _____

Item _____ Size _____ Make _____

Date Acquired _____ Cost _____

Item _____ Size _____ Make _____

Date Acquired _____ Cost _____

Item _____ Size _____ Make _____

Date Acquired _____ Cost _____

Item _____ Size _____ Make _____

Date Acquired _____ Cost _____

Item _____ Size _____ Make _____

Date Acquired _____ Cost _____

Item _____ Size _____ Make _____

Date Acquired _____ Cost _____

• LUGGAGE •

Suitcases, Makeup Cases, Briefcases, Attache Cases, Suit Bags, etc.

Item _____ Size _____ Make _____

Date Acquired _____ Cost _____

Item _____ Size _____ Make _____

Date Acquired _____ Cost _____

Item _____ Size _____ Make _____

Date Acquired _____ Cost _____

Item _____ Size _____ Make _____

Date Acquired _____ Cost _____

Item _____ Size _____ Make _____

Date Acquired _____ Cost _____

Item _____ Size _____ Make _____

Date Acquired _____ Cost _____

Item _____ Size _____ Make _____

Date Acquired _____ Cost _____

Item _____ Size _____ Make _____

Date Acquired _____ Cost _____

Item _____ Size _____ Make _____

Date Acquired _____ Cost _____

Item _____ Size _____ Make _____

Date Acquired _____ Cost _____

Item _____ Size _____ Make _____

Date Acquired _____ Cost _____

Item _____ Size _____ Make _____

Date Acquired _____ Cost _____

Item _____ Size _____ Make _____

Date Acquired _____ Cost _____

Item _____ Size _____ Make _____

Date Acquired _____ Cost _____

Item _____ Size _____ Make _____

Date Acquired _____ Cost _____

Item _____ Size _____ Make _____

Date Acquired _____ Cost _____

Item _____ Size _____ Make _____

Date Acquired _____ Cost _____

Item _____ Size _____ Make _____

Date Acquired _____ Cost _____

Item _____ Size _____ Make _____

Date Acquired _____ Cost _____

Item _____ Size _____ Make _____

Date Acquired _____ Cost _____

Item _____ Size _____ Make _____

Date Acquired _____ Cost _____

• SPORTING EQUIPMENT •

Golf Clubs, Bicycles, Skis, Boats, Packboards, Tennis Rackets, Bowling Balls, Baseball Gloves, etc.

Item _____ Size _____ Make _____

Model No. _____ Serial No. _____ Date Acquired _____ Cost _____

Item _____ Size _____ Make _____

Model No. _____ Serial No. _____ Date Acquired _____ Cost _____

Item _____ Size _____ Make _____

Model No. _____ Serial No. _____ Date Acquired _____ Cost _____

Item _____ Size _____ Make _____

Model No. _____ Serial No. _____ Date Acquired _____ Cost _____

Item _____ Size _____ Make _____

Model No. _____ Serial No. _____ Date Acquired _____ Cost _____

Item _____ Size _____ Make _____

Model No. _____ Serial No. _____ Date Acquired _____ Cost _____

Item _____ Size _____ Make _____

Model No. _____ Serial No. _____ Date Acquired _____ Cost _____

Item _____ Size _____ Make _____

Model No. _____ Serial No. _____ Date Acquired _____ Cost _____

Item _____ Size _____ Make _____

Model No. _____ Serial No. _____ Date Acquired _____ Cost _____

Item _____ Size _____ Make _____

Model No. _____ Serial No. _____ Date Acquired _____ Cost _____

Item _____ Size _____ Make _____

Model No. _____ Serial No. _____ Date Acquired _____ Cost _____

Item _____ Size _____ Make _____

Model No. _____ Serial No. _____ Date Acquired _____ Cost _____

Item _____ Size _____ Make _____

Model No. _____ Serial No. _____ Date Acquired _____ Cost _____

Item _____ Size _____ Make _____

Model No. _____ Serial No. _____ Date Acquired _____ Cost _____

Item _____ Size _____ Make _____

Model No. _____ Serial No. _____ Date Acquired _____ Cost _____

Item _____ Size _____ Make _____

Model No. _____ Serial No. _____ Date Acquired _____ Cost _____

Item _____ Size _____ Make _____

Model No. _____ Serial No. _____ Date Acquired _____ Cost _____

Item _____ Size _____ Make _____

Model No. _____ Serial No. _____ Date Acquired _____ Cost _____

Item _____ Size _____ Make _____

Model No. _____ Serial No. _____ Date Acquired _____ Cost _____

Item _____ Size _____ Make _____

Model No. _____ Serial No. _____ Date Acquired _____ Cost _____

Item _____ Size _____ Make _____

Model No. _____ Serial No. _____ Date Acquired _____ Cost _____

Item _____ Size _____ Make _____

Model No. _____ Serial No. _____ Date Acquired _____ Cost _____

Item _____ Size _____ Make _____

Model No. _____ Serial No. _____ Date Acquired _____ Cost _____

Item _____ Size _____ Make _____

Model No. _____ Serial No. _____ Date Acquired _____ Cost _____

Item _____ Size _____ Make _____

Model No. _____ Serial No. _____ Date Acquired _____ Cost _____

Item _____ Size _____ Make _____

Model No. _____ Serial No. _____ Date Acquired _____ Cost _____

Item _____ Size _____ Make _____

Model No. _____ Serial No. _____ Date Acquired _____ Cost _____

Item _____ Size _____ Make _____

Model No. _____ Serial No. _____ Date Acquired _____ Cost _____

Item _____ Size _____ Make _____

Model No. _____ Serial No. _____ Date Acquired _____ Cost _____

Item _____ Size _____ Make _____

Model No. _____ Serial No. _____ Date Acquired _____ Cost _____

Item _____ Size _____ Make _____

Model No. _____ Serial No. _____ Date Acquired _____ Cost _____

Item _____ Size _____ Make _____

Model No. _____ Serial No. _____ Date Acquired _____ Cost _____

Item _____ Size _____ Make _____

Model No. _____ Serial No. _____ Date Acquired _____ Cost _____

Item _____ Size _____ Make _____

Model No. _____ Serial No. _____ Date Acquired _____ Cost _____

Item _____ Size _____ Make _____

Model No. _____ Serial No. _____ Date Acquired _____ Cost _____

Item _____ Size _____ Make _____

Model No. _____ Serial No. _____ Date Acquired _____ Cost _____

Item _____ Size _____ Make _____

Model No. _____ Serial No. _____ Date Acquired _____ Cost _____

Item _____ Size _____ Make _____

Model No. _____ Serial No. _____ Date Acquired _____ Cost _____

Item _____ Size _____ Make _____

Model No. _____ Serial No. _____ Date Acquired _____ Cost _____

• BOOKS, RECORDS & TAPES •

Item _____ Title _____ Date Acquired _____

Cost _____ Publisher _____

Item _____ Title _____ Date Acquired _____

Cost _____ Publisher _____

Item _____ Title _____ Date Acquired _____

Cost _____ Publisher _____

Item _____ Title _____ Date Acquired _____

Cost _____ Publisher _____

Item _____ Title _____ Date Acquired _____

Cost _____ Publisher _____

Item _____ Title _____ Date Acquired _____

Cost _____ Publisher _____

Item _____ Title _____ Date Acquired _____

Cost _____ Publisher _____

Item _____ Title _____ Date Acquired _____

Cost _____ Publisher _____

Item _____ Title _____ Date Acquired _____

Cost _____ Publisher _____

Item _____ Title _____ Date Acquired _____

Cost _____ Publisher _____

Item _____ Title _____ Date Acquired _____

Cost _____ Publisher _____

Item _____ Title _____ Date Acquired _____

Cost _____ Publisher _____

Item _____ Title _____ Date Acquired _____

Cost _____ Publisher _____

Item _____ Title _____ Date Acquired _____

Cost _____ Publisher _____

Item _____ Title _____ Date Acquired _____

Cost _____ Publisher _____

Item _____ Title _____ Date Acquired _____

Cost _____ Publisher _____

Item _____ Title _____ Date Acquired _____

Cost _____ Publisher _____

Item _____ Title _____ Date Acquired _____

Cost _____ Publisher _____

Item _____ Title _____ Date Acquired _____

Cost _____ Publisher _____

Item _____ Title _____ Date Acquired _____

Cost _____ Publisher _____

Item _____ Title _____ Date Acquired _____

Cost _____ Publisher _____

Item _____ Title _____ Date Acquired _____

Cost _____ Publisher _____

Item _____ Title _____ Date Acquired _____

Cost _____ Publisher _____

Item _____ Title _____ Date Acquired _____

Cost _____ Publisher _____

Item _____ Title _____ Date Acquired _____

Cost _____ Publisher _____

Item _____ Title _____ Date Acquired _____

Cost _____ Publisher _____

Item _____ Title _____ Date Acquired _____

Cost _____ Publisher _____

Item _____ Title _____ Date Acquired _____

Cost _____ Publisher _____

Item _____ Title _____ Date Acquired _____

Cost _____ Publisher _____

Item _____ Title _____ Date Acquired _____

Cost _____ Publisher _____

Item _____ Title _____ Date Acquired _____

Cost _____ Publisher _____

Item _____ Title _____ Date Acquired _____

Cost _____ Publisher _____

Item _____ Title _____ Date Acquired _____

Cost _____ Publisher _____

Item _____ Title _____ Date Acquired _____

Cost _____ Publisher _____

Item _____ Title _____ Date Acquired _____

Cost _____ Publisher _____

Item _____ Title _____ Date Acquired _____

Cost _____ Publisher _____

Item _____ Title _____ Date Acquired _____

Cost _____ Publisher _____

Item _____ Title _____ Date Acquired _____

Cost _____ Publisher _____

Item _____ Title _____ Date Acquired _____

Cost _____ Publisher _____

• EXPENSIVE CLOTHING •

Suits, Dresses, Overcoats, Shoes, Hats, etc.

Item _____ Material _____ Size _____ Make _____

Color _____ Date Acquired _____ Cost _____

Item _____ Material _____ Size _____ Make _____

Color _____ Date Acquired _____ Cost _____

Item _____ Material _____ Size _____ Make _____

Color _____ Date Acquired _____ Cost _____

Item _____ Material _____ Size _____ Make _____

Color _____ Date Acquired _____ Cost _____

Item _____ Material _____ Size _____ Make _____

Color _____ Date Acquired _____ Cost _____

Item _____ Material _____ Size _____ Make _____

Color _____ Date Acquired _____ Cost _____

Item _____ Material _____ Size _____ Make _____

Color _____ Date Acquired _____ Cost _____

Item _____ Material _____ Size _____ Make _____

Color _____ Date Acquired _____ Cost _____

Item _____ Material _____ Size _____ Make _____

Color _____ Date Acquired _____ Cost _____

Item _____ Material _____ Size _____ Make _____

Color _____ Date Acquired _____ Cost _____

Item _____ Material _____ Size _____ Make _____

Color _____ Date Acquired _____ Cost _____

Item _____ Material _____ Size _____ Make _____

Color _____ Date Acquired _____ Cost _____

Item _____ Material _____ Size _____ Make _____

Color _____ Date Acquired _____ Cost _____

Item _____ Material _____ Size _____ Make _____

Color _____ Date Acquired _____ Cost _____

Item _____ Material _____ Size _____ Make _____

Color _____ Date Acquired _____ Cost _____

Item _____ Material _____ Size _____ Make _____

Color _____ Date Acquired _____ Cost _____

Item _____ Material _____ Size _____ Make _____

Color _____ Date Acquired _____ Cost _____

Item _____ Material _____ Size _____ Make _____

Color _____ Date Acquired _____ Cost _____

Item _____ Material _____ Size _____ Make _____

Color _____ Date Acquired _____ Cost _____

Item _____ Material _____ Size _____ Make _____

Color _____ Date Acquired _____ Cost _____

Item _____ Material _____ Size _____ Make _____

Color _____ Date Acquired _____ Cost _____

Item _____ Material _____ Size _____ Make _____

Color _____ Date Acquired _____ Cost _____

Item _____ Material _____ Size _____ Make _____

Color _____ Date Acquired _____ Cost _____

Item _____ Material _____ Size _____ Make _____

Color _____ Date Acquired _____ Cost _____

Item _____ Material _____ Size _____ Make _____

Color _____ Date Acquired _____ Cost _____

Item _____ Material _____ Size _____ Make _____

Color _____ Date Acquired _____ Cost _____

Item _____ Material _____ Size _____ Make _____

Color _____ Date Acquired _____ Cost _____

Item _____ Material _____ Size _____ Make _____

Color _____ Date Acquired _____ Cost _____

Item _____ Material _____ Size _____ Make _____

Color _____ Date Acquired _____ Cost _____

Item _____ Material _____ Size _____ Make _____

Color _____ Date Acquired _____ Cost _____

Item _____ Material _____ Size _____ Make _____

Color _____ Date Acquired _____ Cost _____

Item _____ Material _____ Size _____ Make _____

Color _____ Date Acquired _____ Cost _____

Item _____ Material _____ Size _____ Make _____

Color _____ Date Acquired _____ Cost _____

Item _____ Material _____ Size _____ Make _____

Color _____ Date Acquired _____ Cost _____

Item _____ Material _____ Size _____ Make _____

Color _____ Date Acquired _____ Cost _____

Item _____ Material _____ Size _____ Make _____

Color _____ Date Acquired _____ Cost _____

Item _____ Material _____ Size _____ Make _____

Color _____ Date Acquired _____ Cost _____

Item _____ Material _____ Size _____ Make _____

Color _____ Date Acquired _____ Cost _____

Item _____ Material _____ Size _____ Make _____

Color _____ Date Acquired _____ Cost _____

• FURS •

Item _____ Material _____ Size _____ Make _____

Color _____ Date Acquired _____ Cost _____

Item _____ Material _____ Size _____ Make _____

Color _____ Date Acquired _____ Cost _____

Item _____ Material _____ Size _____ Make _____

Color _____ Date Acquired _____ Cost _____

Item _____ Material _____ Size _____ Make _____

Color _____ Date Acquired _____ Cost _____

Item _____ Material _____ Size _____ Make _____

Color _____ Date Acquired _____ Cost _____

Item _____ Material _____ Size _____ Make _____

Color _____ Date Acquired _____ Cost _____

Item _____ Material _____ Size _____ Make _____

Color _____ Date Acquired _____ Cost _____

Item _____ Material _____ Size _____ Make _____

Color _____ Date Acquired _____ Cost _____

Item _____ Material _____ Size _____ Make _____

Color _____ Date Acquired _____ Cost _____

Item _____ Material _____ Size _____ Make _____

Color _____ Date Acquired _____ Cost _____

Item _____ Material _____ Size _____ Make _____

Color _____ Date Acquired _____ Cost _____

Item _____ Material _____ Size _____ Make _____

Color _____ Date Acquired _____ Cost _____

Item _____ Material _____ Size _____ Make _____

Color _____ Date Acquired _____ Cost _____

Item _____ Material _____ Size _____ Make _____

Color _____ Date Acquired _____ Cost _____

Item _____ Material _____ Size _____ Make _____

Color _____ Date Acquired _____ Cost _____

Item _____ Material _____ Size _____ Make _____

Color _____ Date Acquired _____ Cost _____

Item _____ Material _____ Size _____ Make _____

Color _____ Date Acquired _____ Cost _____

Item _____ Material _____ Size _____ Make _____

Color _____ Date Acquired _____ Cost _____

Item _____ Material _____ Size _____ Make _____

Color _____ Date Acquired _____ Cost _____

Item _____ Material _____ Size _____ Make _____

Color _____ Date Acquired _____ Cost _____

Item _____ Material _____ Size _____ Make _____

Color _____ Date Acquired _____ Cost _____

Item _____ Material _____ Size _____ Make _____

Color _____ Date Acquired _____ Cost _____

Item _____ Material _____ Size _____ Make _____

Color _____ Date Acquired _____ Cost _____

Item _____ Material _____ Size _____ Make _____

Color _____ Date Acquired _____ Cost _____

Item _____ Material _____ Size _____ Make _____

Color _____ Date Acquired _____ Cost _____

Item _____ Material _____ Size _____ Make _____

Color _____ Date Acquired _____ Cost _____

Item _____ Material _____ Size _____ Make _____

Color _____ Date Acquired _____ Cost _____

Item _____ Material _____ Size _____ Make _____

Color _____ Date Acquired _____ Cost _____

• JEWELRY •

Rings, Necklaces, Earrings, Bracelets, Unset Gems, Chains, Watches, etc.

Item _____ Material _____ Make _____

Date Acquired _____ Cost _____

Item _____ Material _____ Make _____

Date Acquired _____ Cost _____

Item _____ Material _____ Make _____

Date Acquired _____ Cost _____

Item _____ Material _____ Make _____

Date Acquired _____ Cost _____

Item _____ Material _____ Make _____

Date Acquired _____ Cost _____

Item _____ Material _____ Make _____

Date Acquired _____ Cost _____

Item _____ Material _____ Make _____

Date Acquired _____ Cost _____

Item _____ Material _____ Make _____

Date Acquired _____ Cost _____

Item _____ Material _____ Make _____

Date Acquired _____ Cost _____

Item _____ Material _____ Make _____

Date Acquired _____ Cost _____

Item _____ Material _____ Make _____

Date Acquired _____ Cost _____

Item _____ Material _____ Make _____

Date Acquired _____ Cost _____

Item _____ Material _____ Make _____

Date Acquired _____ Cost _____

Item _____ Material _____ Make _____

Date Acquired _____ Cost _____

Item _____ Material _____ Make _____

Date Acquired _____ Cost _____

Item _____ Material _____ Make _____

Date Acquired _____ Cost _____

Item _____ Material _____ Make _____

Date Acquired _____ Cost _____

Item _____ Material _____ Make _____

Date Acquired _____ Cost _____

Item _____ Material _____ Make _____

Date Acquired _____ Cost _____

Item _____ Material _____ Make _____

Date Acquired _____ Cost _____

Item _____ Material _____ Make _____

Date Acquired _____ Cost _____

Item _____ Material _____ Make _____

Date Acquired _____ Cost _____

Item _____ Material _____ Make _____

Date Acquired _____ Cost _____

Item _____ Material _____ Make _____

Date Acquired _____ Cost _____

Item _____ Material _____ Make _____

Date Acquired _____ Cost _____

Item _____ Material _____ Make _____

Date Acquired _____ Cost _____

Item _____ Material _____ Make _____

Date Acquired _____ Cost _____

Item _____ Material _____ Make _____

Date Acquired _____ Cost _____

Item _____ Material _____ Make _____

Date Acquired _____ Cost _____

Item _____ Material _____ Make _____

Date Acquired _____ Cost _____

Item _____ Material _____ Make _____

Date Acquired _____ Cost _____

Item _____ Material _____ Make _____

Date Acquired _____ Cost _____

Item _____ Material _____ Make _____

Date Acquired _____ Cost _____

Item _____ Material _____ Make _____

Date Acquired _____ Cost _____

Item _____ Material _____ Make _____

Date Acquired _____ Cost _____

Item _____ Material _____ Make _____

Date Acquired _____ Cost _____

Item _____ Material _____ Make _____

Date Acquired _____ Cost _____

Item _____ Material _____ Make _____

Date Acquired _____ Cost _____

Item _____ Material _____ Make _____

Date Acquired _____ Cost _____

Item _____ Material _____ Make _____

Date Acquired _____ Cost _____

• COLLECTIBLES •

Antiques, Coins, Stamps, Dolls, Matchbook Covers, Cigar Box Labels, Comic Books, etc.

Item _____ Date Acquired _____ Cost _____

Item _____ Date Acquired _____ Cost _____

Item _____ Date Acquired _____ Cost _____

Item _____ Date Acquired _____ Cost _____

Item _____ Date Acquired _____ Cost _____

Item _____ Date Acquired _____ Cost _____

Item _____ Date Acquired _____ Cost _____

Item _____ Date Acquired _____ Cost _____

Item _____ Date Acquired _____ Cost _____

Item _____ Date Acquired _____ Cost _____

Item _____ Date Acquired _____ Cost _____

Item _____ Date Acquired _____ Cost _____

Item _____ Date Acquired _____ Cost _____

Item _____ Date Acquired _____ Cost _____

Item _____ Date Acquired _____ Cost _____

Item _____ Date Acquired _____ Cost _____

Item _____ Date Acquired _____ Cost _____

Item _____ Date Acquired _____ Cost _____

Item _____ Date Acquired _____ Cost _____

Item _____ Date Acquired _____ Cost _____

Item _____ Date Acquired _____ Cost _____

Item _____ Date Acquired _____ Cost _____

Item _____ Date Acquired _____ Cost _____

Item _____ Date Acquired _____ Cost _____

Item _____ Date Acquired _____ Cost _____

Item _____ Date Acquired _____ Cost _____

Item _____ Date Acquired _____ Cost _____

Item _____ Date Acquired _____ Cost _____

Item _____ Date Acquired _____ Cost _____

Item _____ Date Acquired _____ Cost _____

Item _____ Date Acquired _____ Cost _____

Item _____ Date Acquired _____ Cost _____

Item _____ Date Acquired _____ Cost _____

Item _____ Date Acquired _____ Cost _____

Item _____ Date Acquired _____ Cost _____

Item _____ Date Acquired _____ Cost _____

Item _____ Date Acquired _____ Cost _____

Item _____ Date Acquired _____ Cost _____

Item _____ Date Acquired _____ Cost _____

Item _____ Date Acquired _____ Cost _____

Item _____ Date Acquired _____ Cost _____

Item _____ Date Acquired _____ Cost _____

Item _____ Date Acquired _____ Cost _____

Item _____ Date Acquired _____ Cost _____

Item _____ Date Acquired _____ Cost _____

Item _____ Date Acquired _____ Cost _____

Item _____ Date Acquired _____ Cost _____

Item _____ Date Acquired _____ Cost _____

Item _____ Date Acquired _____ Cost _____

Item _____ Date Acquired _____ Cost _____

Item _____ Date Acquired _____ Cost _____

Item _____ Date Acquired _____ Cost _____

Item _____ Date Acquired _____ Cost _____

Item _____ Date Acquired _____ Cost _____

Item _____ Date Acquired _____ Cost _____

Item _____ Date Acquired _____ Cost _____

Item _____ Date Acquired _____ Cost _____

Item _____ Date Acquired _____ Cost _____

Item _____ Date Acquired _____ Cost _____

Item _____ Date Acquired _____ Cost _____

Item _____ Date Acquired _____ Cost _____

Item _____ Date Acquired _____ Cost _____

Item _____ Date Acquired _____ Cost _____

Item _____ Date Acquired _____ Cost _____

Item _____ Date Acquired _____ Cost _____

Item _____ Date Acquired _____ Cost _____

Item _____ Date Acquired _____ Cost _____

Item _____ Date Acquired _____ Cost _____

Item _____ Date Acquired _____ Cost _____

Item _____ Date Acquired _____ Cost _____

Item _____ Date Acquired _____ Cost _____

Item _____ Date Acquired _____ Cost _____

Item _____ Date Acquired _____ Cost _____

Item _____ Date Acquired _____ Cost _____

Item _____ Date Acquired _____ Cost _____

Item _____ Date Acquired _____ Cost _____

Item _____ Date Acquired _____ Cost _____

Item _____ Date Acquired _____ Cost _____

Item _____ Date Acquired _____ Cost _____

Item _____ Date Acquired _____ Cost _____

Item _____ Date Acquired _____ Cost _____

Item _____ Date Acquired _____ Cost _____

Item _____ Date Acquired _____ Cost _____

Item _____ Date Acquired _____ Cost _____

Item _____ Date Acquired _____ Cost _____

Item _____ Date Acquired _____ Cost _____

Item _____ Date Acquired _____ Cost _____

Item _____ Date Acquired _____ Cost _____

Item _____ Date Acquired _____ Cost _____

Item _____ Date Acquired _____ Cost _____

Item _____ Date Acquired _____ Cost _____

Item _____ Date Acquired _____ Cost _____

Item _____ Date Acquired _____ Cost _____

Item _____ Date Acquired _____ Cost _____

• PAINTINGS & SCULPTURE •

Item _____ Title _____ Artist _____

Frame or Mounting _____ Date Acquired _____ Cost _____

Item _____ Title _____ Artist _____

Frame or Mounting _____ Date Acquired _____ Cost _____

Item _____ Title _____ Artist _____

Frame or Mounting _____ Date Acquired _____ Cost _____

Item _____ Title _____ Artist _____

Frame or Mounting _____ Date Acquired _____ Cost _____

Item _____ Title _____ Artist _____

Frame or Mounting _____ Date Acquired _____ Cost _____

Item _____ Title _____ Artist _____

Frame or Mounting _____ Date Acquired _____ Cost _____

Item _____ Title _____ Artist _____

Frame or Mounting _____ Date Acquired _____ Cost _____

Item _____ Title _____ Artist _____

Frame or Mounting _____ Date Acquired _____ Cost _____

Item _____ Title _____ Artist _____

Frame or Mounting _____ Date Acquired _____ Cost _____

Item _____ Title _____ Artist _____

Frame or Mounting _____ Date Acquired _____ Cost _____

Item _____ Title _____ Artist _____

Frame or Mounting _____ Date Acquired _____ Cost _____

Item _____ Title _____ Artist _____

Frame or Mounting _____ Date Acquired _____ Cost _____

Item _____ Title _____ Artist _____

Frame or Mounting _____ Date Acquired _____ Cost _____

Item _____ Title _____ Artist _____

Frame or Mounting _____ Date Acquired _____ Cost _____

Item _____ Title _____ Artist _____

Frame or Mounting _____ Date Acquired _____ Cost _____

Item _____ Title _____ Artist _____

Frame or Mounting _____ Date Acquired _____ Cost _____

Item _____ Title _____ Artist _____

Frame or Mounting _____ Date Acquired _____ Cost _____

Item _____ Title _____ Artist _____

Frame or Mounting _____ Date Acquired _____ Cost _____

Item _____ Title _____ Artist _____

Frame or Mounting _____ Date Acquired _____ Cost _____

• RARE CARPETS & TAPESTRIES •

Item _____ Size _____ Color _____

Material _____ Date Acquired _____ Cost _____

Item _____ Size _____ Color _____

Material _____ Date Acquired _____ Cost _____

Item _____ Size _____ Color _____

Material _____ Date Acquired _____ Cost _____

Item _____ Size _____ Color _____

Material _____ Date Acquired _____ Cost _____

Item _____ Size _____ Color _____

Material _____ Date Acquired _____ Cost _____

Item _____ Size _____ Color _____

Material _____ Date Acquired _____ Cost _____

Item _____ Size _____ Color _____

Material _____ Date Acquired _____ Cost _____

Item _____ Size _____ Color _____

Material _____ Date Acquired _____ Cost _____

Item _____ Size _____ Color _____

Material _____ Date Acquired _____ Cost _____

Item _____ Size _____ Color _____

Material _____ Date Acquired _____ Cost _____

Item _____ Size _____ Color _____

Material _____ Date Acquired _____ Cost _____

Item _____ Size _____ Color _____

Material _____ Date Acquired _____ Cost _____

Item _____ Size _____ Color _____

Material _____ Date Acquired _____ Cost _____

Item _____ Size _____ Color _____

Material _____ Date Acquired _____ Cost _____

Item _____ Size _____ Color _____

Material _____ Date Acquired _____ Cost _____

Item _____ Size _____ Color _____

Material _____ Date Acquired _____ Cost _____

Item _____ Size _____ Color _____

Material _____ Date Acquired _____ Cost _____

Item _____ Size _____ Color _____

Material _____ Date Acquired _____ Cost _____

Item _____ Size _____ Color _____

Material _____ Date Acquired _____ Cost _____

• SILVERWARE, CHINA, GLASS •

Item _____ Size _____ Pattern _____

Make _____ Date Acquired _____ Cost _____

Item _____ Size _____ Pattern _____

Make _____ Date Acquired _____ Cost _____

Item _____ Size _____ Pattern _____

Make _____ Date Acquired _____ Cost _____

Item _____ Size _____ Pattern _____

Make _____ Date Acquired _____ Cost _____

Item _____ Size _____ Pattern _____

Make _____ Date Acquired _____ Cost _____

Item _____ Size _____ Pattern _____

Make _____ Date Acquired _____ Cost _____

Item _____ Size _____ Pattern _____

Make _____ Date Acquired _____ Cost _____

Item _____ Size _____ Pattern _____

Make _____ Date Acquired _____ Cost _____

Item _____ Size _____ Pattern _____

Make _____ Date Acquired _____ Cost _____

Item _____ Size _____ Pattern _____

Make _____ Date Acquired _____ Cost _____

Item _____ Size _____ Pattern _____

Make _____ Date Acquired _____ Cost _____

Item _____ Size _____ Pattern _____

Make _____ Date Acquired _____ Cost _____

Item _____ Size _____ Pattern _____

Make _____ Date Acquired _____ Cost _____

Item _____ Size _____ Pattern _____

Make _____ Date Acquired _____ Cost _____

Item _____ Size _____ Pattern _____

Make _____ Date Acquired _____ Cost _____

Item _____ Size _____ Pattern _____

Make _____ Date Acquired _____ Cost _____

Item _____ Size _____ Pattern _____

Make _____ Date Acquired _____ Cost _____

Item _____ Size _____ Pattern _____

Make _____ Date Acquired _____ Cost _____

Item _____ Size _____ Pattern _____

Make _____ Date Acquired _____ Cost _____

Item _____ Size _____ Pattern _____

Make _____ Date Acquired _____ Cost _____

Item _____ Size _____ Pattern _____

Make _____ Date Acquired _____ Cost _____

Item _____ Size _____ Pattern _____

Make _____ Date Acquired _____ Cost _____

Item _____ Size _____ Pattern _____

Make _____ Date Acquired _____ Cost _____

Item _____ Size _____ Pattern _____

Make _____ Date Acquired _____ Cost _____

Item _____ Size _____ Pattern _____

Make _____ Date Acquired _____ Cost _____

Item _____ Size _____ Pattern _____

Make _____ Date Acquired _____ Cost _____

Item _____ Size _____ Pattern _____

Make _____ Date Acquired _____ Cost _____

Item _____ Size _____ Pattern _____

Make _____ Date Acquired _____ Cost _____

Item _____ Size _____ Pattern _____

Make _____ Date Acquired _____ Cost _____

Item _____ Size _____ Pattern _____

Make _____ Date Acquired _____ Cost _____

Item _____ Size _____ Pattern _____

Make _____ Date Acquired _____ Cost _____

Item _____ Size _____ Pattern _____

Make _____ Date Acquired _____ Cost _____

Item _____ Size _____ Pattern _____

Make _____ Date Acquired _____ Cost _____

Item _____ Size _____ Pattern _____

Make _____ Date Acquired _____ Cost _____

Item _____ Size _____ Pattern _____

Make _____ Date Acquired _____ Cost _____

Item _____ Size _____ Pattern _____

Make _____ Date Acquired _____ Cost _____

Item _____ Size _____ Pattern _____

Make _____ Date Acquired _____ Cost _____

Item _____ Size _____ Pattern _____

Make _____ Date Acquired _____ Cost _____

Item _____ Size _____ Pattern _____

Make _____ Date Acquired _____ Cost _____

Item _____ Size _____ Pattern _____

Make _____ Date Acquired _____ Cost _____

Item _____ Size _____ Pattern _____

Make _____ Date Acquired _____ Cost _____

Item _____ Size _____ Pattern _____

Make _____ Date Acquired _____ Cost _____

Item _____ Size _____ Pattern _____

Make _____ Date Acquired _____ Cost _____

Item _____ Size _____ Pattern _____

Make _____ Date Acquired _____ Cost _____

Item _____ Size _____ Pattern _____

Make _____ Date Acquired _____ Cost _____

Item _____ Size _____ Pattern _____

Make _____ Date Acquired _____ Cost _____

Item _____ Size _____ Pattern _____

Make _____ Date Acquired _____ Cost _____

Item _____ Size _____ Pattern _____

Make _____ Date Acquired _____ Cost _____

Item _____ Size _____ Pattern _____

Make _____ Date Acquired _____ Cost _____

Item _____ Size _____ Pattern _____

Make _____ Date Acquired _____ Cost _____

• FURNITURE & FURNISHINGS •

Living Room (Chairs, Tables, Chests, Lamps, Desks, Stools, Sofas, Carpets, etc.)

Item _____ Material _____ Color _____

Make _____ Date Acquired _____ Cost _____

Item _____ Material _____ Color _____

Make _____ Date Acquired _____ Cost _____

Item _____ Material _____ Color _____

Make _____ Date Acquired _____ Cost _____

Item _____ Material _____ Color _____

Make _____ Date Acquired _____ Cost _____

Item _____ Material _____ Color _____

Make _____ Date Acquired _____ Cost _____

Item _____ Material _____ Color _____

Make _____ Date Acquired _____ Cost _____

Item _____ Material _____ Color _____

Make _____ Date Acquired _____ Cost _____

Item _____ Material _____ Color _____

Make _____ Date Acquired _____ Cost _____

Item _____ Material _____ Color _____

Make _____ Date Acquired _____ Cost _____

Item _____ Material _____ Color _____

Make _____ Date Acquired _____ Cost _____

Item _____ Material _____ Color _____

Make _____ Date Acquired _____ Cost _____

Item _____ Material _____ Color _____

Make _____ Date Acquired _____ Cost _____

Item _____ Material _____ Color _____

Make _____ Date Acquired _____ Cost _____

Item _____ Material _____ Color _____

Make _____ Date Acquired _____ Cost _____

Item _____ Material _____ Color _____

Make _____ Date Acquired _____ Cost _____

Item _____ Material _____ Color _____

Make _____ Date Acquired _____ Cost _____

Item _____ Material _____ Color _____

Make _____ Date Acquired _____ Cost _____

Item _____ Material _____ Color _____

Make _____ Date Acquired _____ Cost _____

Item _____ Material _____ Color _____

Make _____ Date Acquired _____ Cost _____

Item _____ Material _____ Color _____

Make _____ Date Acquired _____ Cost _____

Item _____ Material _____ Color _____

Make _____ Date Acquired _____ Cost _____

Item _____ Material _____ Color _____

Make _____ Date Acquired _____ Cost _____

Item _____ Material _____ Color _____

Make _____ Date Acquired _____ Cost _____

Item _____ Material _____ Color _____

Make _____ Date Acquired _____ Cost _____

Item _____ Material _____ Color _____

Make _____ Date Acquired _____ Cost _____

Item _____ Material _____ Color _____

Make _____ Date Acquired _____ Cost _____

Item _____ Material _____ Color _____

Make _____ Date Acquired _____ Cost _____

Item _____ Material _____ Color _____

Make _____ Date Acquired _____ Cost _____

Item _____ Material _____ Color _____

Make _____ Date Acquired _____ Cost _____

Item _____ Material _____ Color _____

Make _____ Date Acquired _____ Cost _____

Item _____ Material _____ Color _____

Make _____ Date Acquired _____ Cost _____

Item _____ Material _____ Color _____

Make _____ Date Acquired _____ Cost _____

Item _____ Material _____ Color _____

Make _____ Date Acquired _____ Cost _____

Item _____ Material _____ Color _____

Make _____ Date Acquired _____ Cost _____

Item _____ Material _____ Color _____

Make _____ Date Acquired _____ Cost _____

Item _____ Material _____ Color _____

Make _____ Date Acquired _____ Cost _____

Item _____ Material _____ Color _____

Make _____ Date Acquired _____ Cost _____

Item _____ Material _____ Color _____

Make _____ Date Acquired _____ Cost _____

Item _____ Material _____ Color _____

Make _____ Date Acquired _____ Cost _____

• FURNITURE & FURNISHINGS •

Dining Room (Chairs, Tables, Sideboards, Buffets, Serving Carts, Chandeliers, Carpets, Lamps, etc.)

Item _____ Material _____ Color _____

Make _____ Date Acquired _____ Cost _____

Item _____ Material _____ Color _____

Make _____ Date Acquired _____ Cost _____

Item _____ Material _____ Color _____

Make _____ Date Acquired _____ Cost _____

Item _____ Material _____ Color _____

Make _____ Date Acquired _____ Cost _____

Item _____ Material _____ Color _____

Make _____ Date Acquired _____ Cost _____

Item _____ Material _____ Color _____

Make _____ Date Acquired _____ Cost _____

Item _____ Material _____ Color _____

Make _____ Date Acquired _____ Cost _____

Item _____ Material _____ Color _____

Make _____ Date Acquired _____ Cost _____

Item _____ Material _____ Color _____

Make _____ Date Acquired _____ Cost _____

Item _____ Material _____ Color _____

Make _____ Date Acquired _____ Cost _____

Item _____ Material _____ Color _____

Make _____ Date Acquired _____ Cost _____

Item _____ Material _____ Color _____

Make _____ Date Acquired _____ Cost _____

Item _____ Material _____ Color _____

Make _____ Date Acquired _____ Cost _____

Item _____ Material _____ Color _____

Make _____ Date Acquired _____ Cost _____

Item _____ Material _____ Color _____

Make _____ Date Acquired _____ Cost _____

Item _____ Material _____ Color _____

Make _____ Date Acquired _____ Cost _____

Item _____ Material _____ Color _____

Make _____ Date Acquired _____ Cost _____

Item _____ Material _____ Color _____

Make _____ Date Acquired _____ Cost _____

Item _____ Material _____ Color _____

Make _____ Date Acquired _____ Cost _____

Item _____ Material _____ Color _____

Make _____ Date Acquired _____ Cost _____

• FURNITURE & FURNISHINGS •

Family Room (Study, Library, Den) (Chairs, Sofas, Tables, Desks, Lamps, Carpets, Bookcases, Chests, Cabinets, etc.)

Item _____ Material _____ Color _____

Make _____ Date Acquired _____ Cost _____

Item _____ Material _____ Color _____

Make _____ Date Acquired _____ Cost _____

Item _____ Material _____ Color _____

Make _____ Date Acquired _____ Cost _____

Item _____ Material _____ Color _____

Make _____ Date Acquired _____ Cost _____

Item _____ Material _____ Color _____

Make _____ Date Acquired _____ Cost _____

Item _____ Material _____ Color _____

Make _____ Date Acquired _____ Cost _____

Item _____ Material _____ Color _____

Make _____ Date Acquired _____ Cost _____

Item _____ Material _____ Color _____

Make _____ Date Acquired _____ Cost _____

Item _____ Material _____ Color _____

Make _____ Date Acquired _____ Cost _____

Item _____ Material _____ Color _____

Make _____ Date Acquired _____ Cost _____

Item _____ Material _____ Color _____

Make _____ Date Acquired _____ Cost _____

Item _____ Material _____ Color _____

Make _____ Date Acquired _____ Cost _____

'Item _____ Material _____ Color _____

Make _____ Date Acquired _____ Cost _____

Item _____ Material _____ Color _____

Make _____ Date Acquired _____ Cost _____

Item _____ Material _____ Color _____

Make _____ Date Acquired _____ Cost _____

Item _____ Material _____ Color _____

Make _____ Date Acquired _____ Cost _____

Item _____ Material _____ Color _____

Make _____ Date Acquired _____ Cost _____

Item _____ Material _____ Color _____

Make _____ Date Acquired _____ Cost _____

Item _____ Material _____ Color _____

Make _____ Date Acquired _____ Cost _____

Item _____ Material _____ Color _____

Make _____ Date Acquired _____ Cost _____

Item _____ Material _____ Color _____

Make _____ Date Acquired _____ Cost _____

Item _____ Material _____ Color _____

Make _____ Date Acquired _____ Cost _____

Item _____ Material _____ Color _____

Make _____ Date Acquired _____ Cost _____

Item _____ Material _____ Color _____

Make _____ Date Acquired _____ Cost _____

Item _____ Material _____ Color _____

Make _____ Date Acquired _____ Cost _____

Item _____ Material _____ Color _____

Make _____ Date Acquired _____ Cost _____

Item _____ Material _____ Color _____

Make _____ Date Acquired _____ Cost _____

Item _____ Material _____ Color _____

Make _____ Date Acquired _____ Cost _____

Item _____ Material _____ Color _____

Make _____ Date Acquired _____ Cost _____

• FURNITURE & FURNISHINGS •

Bedrooms (Beds, Sofas, Chairs, Tables, Night Stands, Chests, Dressers, Dressing Tables, Lamps, Carpets, Wardrobes, Bookcases, Stools, etc.)

Item _____ Material _____ Color _____

Make _____ Date Acquired _____ Cost _____

Item _____ Material _____ Color _____

Make _____ Date Acquired _____ Cost _____

Item _____ Material _____ Color _____

Make _____ Date Acquired _____ Cost _____

Item _____ Material _____ Color _____

Make _____ Date Acquired _____ Cost _____

Item _____ Material _____ Color _____

Make _____ Date Acquired _____ Cost _____

Item _____ Material _____ Color _____

Make _____ Date Acquired _____ Cost _____

Item _____ Material _____ Color _____

Make _____ Date Acquired _____ Cost _____

Item _____ Material _____ Color _____

Make _____ Date Acquired _____ Cost _____

Item _____ Material _____ Color _____

Make _____ Date Acquired _____ Cost _____

Item _____ Material _____ Color _____

Make _____ Date Acquired _____ Cost _____

Item _____ Material _____ Color _____

Make _____ Date Acquired _____ Cost _____

Item _____ Material _____ Color _____

Make _____ Date Acquired _____ Cost _____

Item _____ Material _____ Color _____

Make _____ Date Acquired _____ Cost _____

Item _____ Material _____ Color _____

Make _____ Date Acquired _____ Cost _____

Item _____ Material _____ Color _____

Make _____ Date Acquired _____ Cost _____

Item _____ Material _____ Color _____

Make _____ Date Acquired _____ Cost _____

Item _____ Material _____ Color _____

Make _____ Date Acquired _____ Cost _____

Item _____ Material _____ Color _____

Make _____ Date Acquired _____ Cost _____

Item _____ Material _____ Color _____

Make _____ Date Acquired _____ Cost _____

Item _____ Material _____ Color _____

Make _____ Date Acquired _____ Cost _____

Item _____ Material _____ Color _____

Make _____ Date Acquired _____ Cost _____

Item _____ Material _____ Color _____

Make _____ Date Acquired _____ Cost _____

Item _____ Material _____ Color _____

Make _____ Date Acquired _____ Cost _____

Item _____ Material _____ Color _____

Make _____ Date Acquired _____ Cost _____

Item _____ Material _____ Color _____

Make _____ Date Acquired _____ Cost _____

Item _____ Material _____ Color _____

Make _____ Date Acquired _____ Cost _____

Item _____ Material _____ Color _____

Make _____ Date Acquired _____ Cost _____

Item _____ Material _____ Color _____

Make _____ Date Acquired _____ Cost _____

Item _____ Material _____ Color _____

Make _____ Date Acquired _____ Cost _____

Item _____ Material _____ Color _____

Make _____ Date Acquired _____ Cost _____

Item _____ Material _____ Color _____

Make _____ Date Acquired _____ Cost _____

Item _____ Material _____ Color _____

Make _____ Date Acquired _____ Cost _____

Item _____ Material _____ Color _____

Make _____ Date Acquired _____ Cost _____

Item _____ Material _____ Color _____

Make _____ Date Acquired _____ Cost _____

Item _____ Material _____ Color _____

Make _____ Date Acquired _____ Cost _____

Item _____ Material _____ Color _____

Make _____ Date Acquired _____ Cost _____

Item _____ Material _____ Color _____

Make _____ Date Acquired _____ Cost _____

Item _____ Material _____ Color _____

Make _____ Date Acquired _____ Cost _____

Item _____ Material _____ Color _____

Make _____ Date Acquired _____ Cost _____

• FURNITURE & FURNISHINGS •

Kitchen & Breakfast Room (Tables, Chairs, Carts, Desks, Cabinets, Carpets, etc.)

Item _____ Material _____ Color _____

Make _____ Date Acquired _____ Cost _____

Item _____ Material _____ Color _____

Make _____ Date Acquired _____ Cost _____

Item _____ Material _____ Color _____

Make _____ Date Acquired _____ Cost _____

Item _____ Material _____ Color _____

Make _____ Date Acquired _____ Cost _____

Item _____ Material _____ Color _____

Make _____ Date Acquired _____ Cost _____

Item _____ Material _____ Color _____

Make _____ Date Acquired _____ Cost _____

Item _____ Material _____ Color _____

Make _____ Date Acquired _____ Cost _____

Item _____ Material _____ Color _____

Make _____ Date Acquired _____ Cost _____

Item _____ Material _____ Color _____

Make _____ Date Acquired _____ Cost _____

Item _____ Material _____ Color _____

Make _____ Date Acquired _____ Cost _____

Item _____ Material _____ Color _____

Make _____ Date Acquired _____ Cost _____

Item _____ Material _____ Color _____

Make _____ Date Acquired _____ Cost _____

Item _____ Material _____ Color _____

Make _____ Date Acquired _____ Cost _____

Item _____ Material _____ Color _____

Make _____ Date Acquired _____ Cost _____

Item _____ Material _____ Color _____

Make _____ Date Acquired _____ Cost _____

Item _____ Material _____ Color _____

Make _____ Date Acquired _____ Cost _____

Item _____ Material _____ Color _____

Make _____ Date Acquired _____ Cost _____

Item _____ Material _____ Color _____

Make _____ Date Acquired _____ Cost _____

Item _____ Material _____ Color _____

Make _____ Date Acquired _____ Cost _____

Item _____ Material _____ Color _____

Make _____ Date Acquired _____ Cost _____

Item _____ Material _____ Color _____

Make _____ Date Acquired _____ Cost _____

Item _____ Material _____ Color _____

Make _____ Date Acquired _____ Cost _____

Item _____ Material _____ Color _____

Make _____ Date Acquired _____ Cost _____

Item _____ Material _____ Color _____

Make _____ Date Acquired _____ Cost _____

Item _____ Material _____ Color _____

Make _____ Date Acquired _____ Cost _____

Item _____ Material _____ Color _____

Make _____ Date Acquired _____ Cost _____

Item _____ Material _____ Color _____

Make _____ Date Acquired _____ Cost _____

Item _____ Material _____ Color _____

Make _____ Date Acquired _____ Cost _____

Item _____ Material _____ Color _____

Make _____ Date Acquired _____ Cost _____

Item _____ Material _____ Color _____

Make _____ Date Acquired _____ Cost _____

Item _____ Material _____ Color _____

Make _____ Date Acquired _____ Cost _____

Item _____ Material _____ Color _____

Make _____ Date Acquired _____ Cost _____

Item _____ Material _____ Color _____

Make _____ Date Acquired _____ Cost _____

Item _____ Material _____ Color _____

Make _____ Date Acquired _____ Cost _____

Item _____ Material _____ Color _____

Make _____ Date Acquired _____ Cost _____

Item _____ Material _____ Color _____

Make _____ Date Acquired _____ Cost _____

Item _____ Material _____ Color _____

Make _____ Date Acquired _____ Cost _____

Item _____ Material _____ Color _____

Make _____ Date Acquired _____ Cost _____

Item _____ Material _____ Color _____

Make _____ Date Acquired _____ Cost _____

• FURNITURE & FURNISHINGS •

Other Rooms

Item _____ Material _____ Color _____

Make _____ Date Acquired _____ Cost _____

Item _____ Material _____ Color _____

Make _____ Date Acquired _____ Cost _____

Item _____ Material _____ Color _____

Make _____ Date Acquired _____ Cost _____

Item _____ Material _____ Color _____

Make _____ Date Acquired _____ Cost _____

Item _____ Material _____ Color _____

Make _____ Date Acquired _____ Cost _____

Item _____ Material _____ Color _____

Make _____ Date Acquired _____ Cost _____

Item _____ Material _____ Color _____

Make _____ Date Acquired _____ Cost _____

Item _____ Material _____ Color _____

Make _____ Date Acquired _____ Cost _____

Item _____ Material _____ Color _____

Make _____ Date Acquired _____ Cost _____

Item _____ Material _____ Color _____

Make _____ Date Acquired _____ Cost _____

Item _____ Material _____ Color _____

Make _____ Date Acquired _____ Cost _____

Item _____ Material _____ Color _____

Make _____ Date Acquired _____ Cost _____

Item _____ Material _____ Color _____

Make _____ Date Acquired _____ Cost _____

Item _____ Material _____ Color _____

Make _____ Date Acquired _____ Cost _____

Item _____ Material _____ Color _____

Make _____ Date Acquired _____ Cost _____

Item _____ Material _____ Color _____

Make _____ Date Acquired _____ Cost _____

Item _____ Material _____ Color _____

Make _____ Date Acquired _____ Cost _____

Item _____ Material _____ Color _____

Make _____ Date Acquired _____ Cost _____

Item _____ Material _____ Color _____

Make _____ Date Acquired _____ Cost _____

Item _____ Material _____ Color _____

Make _____ Date Acquired _____ Cost _____

Item _____ Material _____ Color _____

Make _____ Date Acquired _____ Cost _____

Item _____ Material _____ Color _____

Make _____ Date Acquired _____ Cost _____

Item _____ Material _____ Color _____

Make _____ Date Acquired _____ Cost _____

Item _____ Material _____ Color _____

Make _____ Date Acquired _____ Cost _____

Item _____ Material _____ Color _____

Make _____ Date Acquired _____ Cost _____

Item _____ Material _____ Color _____

Make _____ Date Acquired _____ Cost _____

Item _____ Material _____ Color _____

Make _____ Date Acquired _____ Cost _____

Item _____ Material _____ Color _____

Make _____ Date Acquired _____ Cost _____

Item _____ Material _____ Color _____

Make _____ Date Acquired _____ Cost _____

Item _____ Material _____ Color _____

Make _____ Date Acquired _____ Cost _____

Item _____ Material _____ Color _____

Make _____ Date Acquired _____ Cost _____

Item _____ Material _____ Color _____

Make _____ Date Acquired _____ Cost _____

Item _____ Material _____ Color _____

Make _____ Date Acquired _____ Cost _____

Item _____ Material _____ Color _____

Make _____ Date Acquired _____ Cost _____

Item _____ Material _____ Color _____

Make _____ Date Acquired _____ Cost _____

Item _____ Material _____ Color _____

Make _____ Date Acquired _____ Cost _____

Item _____ Material _____ Color _____

Make _____ Date Acquired _____ Cost _____

Item _____ Material _____ Color _____

Make _____ Date Acquired _____ Cost _____

Item _____ Material _____ Color _____

Make _____ Date Acquired _____ Cost _____

• STORAGE •

Item _____   Material _____   Color _____

Make _____   Date Acquired _____   Cost _____

Item _____   Material _____   Color _____

Make _____   Date Acquired _____   Cost _____

Item _____   Material _____   Color _____

Make _____   Date Acquired _____   Cost _____

Item _____   Material _____   Color _____

Make _____   Date Acquired _____   Cost _____

Item _____   Material _____   Color _____

Make _____   Date Acquired _____   Cost _____

Item _____   Material _____   Color _____

Make _____   Date Acquired _____   Cost _____

Item _____   Material _____   Color _____

Make _____   Date Acquired _____   Cost _____

Item _____   Material _____   Color _____

Make _____   Date Acquired _____   Cost _____

Item _____   Material _____   Color _____

Make _____   Date Acquired _____   Cost _____

Item _____ Material _____ Color _____

Make _____ Date Acquired _____ Cost _____

Item _____ Material _____ Color _____

Make _____ Date Acquired _____ Cost _____

Item _____ Material _____ Color _____

Make _____ Date Acquired _____ Cost _____

Item _____ Material _____ Color _____

Make _____ Date Acquired _____ Cost _____

Item _____ Material _____ Color _____

Make _____ Date Acquired _____ Cost _____

Item _____ Material _____ Color _____

Make _____ Date Acquired _____ Cost _____

Item _____ Material _____ Color _____

Make _____ Date Acquired _____ Cost _____

Item _____ Material _____ Color _____

Make _____ Date Acquired _____ Cost _____

Item _____ Material _____ Color _____

Make _____ Date Acquired _____ Cost _____

Item _____ Material _____ Color _____

Make _____ Date Acquired _____ Cost _____

Item _____ Material _____ Color _____

Make _____ Date Acquired _____ Cost _____

Item _____ Material _____ Color _____

Make _____ Date Acquired _____ Cost _____

Item _____ Material _____ Color _____

Make _____ Date Acquired _____ Cost _____

Item _____ Material _____ Color _____

Make _____ Date Acquired _____ Cost _____

Item _____ Material _____ Color _____

Make _____ Date Acquired _____ Cost _____

Item _____ Material _____ Color _____

Make _____ Date Acquired _____ Cost _____

Item _____ Material _____ Color _____

Make _____ Date Acquired _____ Cost _____

Item _____ Material _____ Color _____

Make _____ Date Acquired _____ Cost _____

Item _____ Material _____ Color _____

Make _____ Date Acquired _____ Cost _____

Item _____ Material _____ Color _____

Make _____ Date Acquired _____ Cost _____

113

Item _____ Material _____ Color _____

Make _____ Date Acquired _____ Cost _____

Item _____ Material _____ Color _____

Make _____ Date Acquired _____ Cost _____

Item _____ Material _____ Color _____

Make _____ Date Acquired _____ Cost _____

'Item _____ Material _____ Color _____

Make _____ Date Acquired _____ Cost _____

Item _____ Material _____ Color _____

Make _____ Date Acquired _____ Cost _____

Item _____ Material _____ Color _____

Make _____ Date Acquired _____ Cost _____

Item _____ Material _____ Color _____

Make _____ Date Acquired _____ Cost _____

Item _____ Material _____ Color _____

Make _____ Date Acquired _____ Cost _____

Item _____ Material _____ Color _____

Make _____ Date Acquired _____ Cost _____

Item _____ Material _____ Color _____

Make _____ Date Acquired _____ Cost _____

• OUTDOOR FURNITURE & PLAY EQUIPMENT •

Chairs, Tables, Umbrellas, Chaises, Porch Swings, Swings, Jungle Jims Slides, Carousels, etc.

Item _____ Material _____ Color _____

Make _____ Date Acquired _____ Cost _____

Item _____ Material _____ Color _____

Make _____ Date Acquired _____ Cost _____

Item _____ Material _____ Color _____

Make _____ Date Acquired _____ Cost _____

Item _____ Material _____ Color _____

Make _____ Date Acquired _____ Cost _____

Item _____ Material _____ Color _____

Make _____ Date Acquired _____ Cost _____

Item _____ Material _____ Color _____

Make _____ Date Acquired _____ Cost _____

Item _____ Material _____ Color _____

Make _____ Date Acquired _____ Cost _____

Item _____ Material _____ Color _____

Make _____ Date Acquired _____ Cost _____

Item _____ Material _____ Color _____

Make _____ Date Acquired _____ Cost _____

Item _____ Material _____ Color _____

Make _____ Date Acquired _____ Cost _____

Item _____ Material _____ Color _____

Make _____ Date Acquired _____ Cost _____

Item _____ Material _____ Color _____

Make _____ Date Acquired _____ Cost _____

Item _____ Material _____ Color _____

Make _____ Date Acquired _____ Cost _____

Item _____ Material _____ Color _____

Make _____ Date Acquired _____ Cost _____

Item _____ Material _____ Color _____

Make _____ Date Acquired _____ Cost _____

Item _____ Material _____ Color _____

Make _____ Date Acquired _____ Cost _____

Item _____ Material _____ Color _____

Make _____ Date Acquired _____ Cost _____

Item _____ Material _____ Color _____

Make _____ Date Acquired _____ Cost _____

Item _____ Material _____ Color _____

Make _____ Date Acquired _____ Cost _____

Item _____ Material _____ Color _____

Make _____ Date Acquired _____ Cost _____

• IMPORTANT PAPERS •

Should be kept in a safe deposit box (Stocks, Bonds, Deeds, Bankbooks, Credit Cards, Mortgages, Birth Certificates, Marriage Certificates, Military Discharges, Naturalization Certificates, Insurance Policies, etc.)

Item _____ Issued to _____

Date Issued _____ Issued by _____ Place Issued _____

Where Kept _____

Item _____ Issued to _____

Date Issued _____ Issued by _____ Place Issued _____

Where Kept _____

Item _____ Issued to _____

Date Issued _____ Issued by _____ Place Issued _____

Where Kept _____

Item _____ Issued to _____

Date Issued _____ Issued by _____ Place Issued _____

Where Kept _____

Item _____ Issued to _____

Date Issued _____ Issued by _____ Place Issued _____

Where Kept _____

Item _____ Issued to _____

Date Issued _____ Issued by _____ Place Issued _____

Where Kept _____

Item _____ Issued to _____

Date Issued _____ Issued by _____ Place Issued _____

Where Kept _____

Item _____ Issued to _____

Date Issued _____ Issued by _____ Place Issued _____

Where Kept _____

Item _____ Issued to _____

Date Issued _____ Issued by _____ Place Issued _____

Where Kept _____

Item _____ Issued to _____

Date Issued _____ Issued by _____ Place Issued _____

Where Kept _____

Item _____ Issued to _____

Date Issued _____ Issued by _____ Place Issued _____

Where Kept _____

Item _____ Issued to _____

Date Issued _____ Issued by _____ Place Issued _____

Where Kept _____

Item _____ Issued to _____

Date Issued _____ Issued by _____ Place Issued _____

Where Kept _____

Item _____ Issued to _____

Date Issued _____ Issued by _____ Place Issued _____

Where Kept _____

Item _____ Issued to _____

Date Issued _____ Issued by _____ Place Issued _____

Where Kept _____

Item _____ Issued to _____

Date Issued _____ Issued by _____ Place Issued _____

Where Kept _____

Item _____ Issued to _____

Date Issued _____ Issued by _____ Place Issued _____

Where Kept _____

Item _____ Issued to _____

Date Issued _____ Issued by _____ Place Issued _____

Where Kept _____

Item _____ Issued to _____

Date Issued _____ Issued by _____ Place Issued _____

Where Kept _____

Item _____ Issued to _____

Date Issued _____ Issued by _____ Place Issued _____

Where Kept _____

Item _____ Issued to _____

Date Issued _____ Issued by _____ Place Issued _____

Where Kept _____

● FIREARMS ●

Rifles, Pistols, Revolvers

Item _____ Make & Model _____ Year _____

Caliber _____ Serial Number _____ Where Purchased _____

Item _____ Make & Model _____ Year _____

Caliber _____ Serial Number _____ Where Purchased _____

Item _____ Make & Model _____ Year _____

Caliber _____ Serial Number _____ Where Purchased _____

Item _____ Make & Model _____ Year _____

Caliber _____ Serial Number _____ Where Purchased _____

Item _____ Make & Model _____ Year _____

Caliber _____ Serial Number _____ Where Purchased _____

Item _____ Make & Model _____ Year _____

Caliber _____ Serial Number _____ Where Purchased _____

Item _____ Make & Model _____ Year _____

Caliber _____ Serial Number _____ Where Purchased _____

Item _____ Make & Model _____ Year _____

Caliber _____ Serial Number _____ Where Purchased _____

Item _____ Make & Model _____ Year _____

Caliber _____ Serial Number _____ Where Purchased _____

Item _____ Make & Model _____ Year _____

Caliber _____ Serial Number _____ Where Purchased _____

Item _____ Make & Model _____ Year _____

Caliber _____ Serial Number _____ Where Purchased _____

Item _____ Make & Model _____ Year _____

Caliber _____ Serial Number _____ Where Purchased _____

Item _____ Make & Model _____ Year _____

Caliber _____ Serial Number _____ Where Purchased _____

Item _____ Make & Model _____ Year _____

Caliber _____ Serial Number _____ Where Purchased _____

Item _____ Make & Model _____ Year _____

Caliber _____ Serial Number _____ Where Purchased _____

Item _____ Make & Model _____ Year _____

Caliber _____ Serial Number _____ Where Purchased _____

Item _____ Make & Model _____ Year _____

Caliber _____ Serial Number _____ Where Purchased _____

Item _____ Make & Model _____ Year _____

Caliber _____ Serial Number _____ Where Purchased _____

Item _____ Make & Model _____ Year _____

Caliber _____ Serial Number _____ Where Purchased _____

Item _____ Make & Model _____ Year _____

Caliber _____ Serial Number _____ Where Purchased _____

Item _____ Make & Model _____ Year _____

Caliber _____ Serial Number _____ Where Purchased _____

Item _____ Make & Model _____ Year _____

Caliber _____ Serial Number _____ Where Purchased _____

Item _____ Make & Model _____ Year _____

Caliber _____ Serial Number _____ Where Purchased _____

Item _____ Make & Model _____ Year _____

Caliber _____ Serial Number _____ Where Purchased _____

Item _____ Make & Model _____ Year _____

Caliber _____ Serial Number _____ Where Purchased _____

Item _____ Make & Model _____ Year _____

Caliber _____ Serial Number _____ Where Purchased _____

Item _____ Make & Model _____ Year _____

Caliber _____ Serial Number _____ Where Purchased _____

Item _____ Make & Model _____ Year _____

Caliber _____ Serial Number _____ Where Purchased _____

Item _____ Make & Model _____ Year _____

Caliber _____ Serial Number _____ Where Purchased _____